Nat___

New Hampshire Lakes Region

An AMC Nature Walks Book

Steve Sherman & Julia Older

APPALACHIAN MOUNTAIN CLUB BOOKS
BOSTON, MASSACHUSETTS

6 52932 01295 0

917.42
0

Cover Photograph: Ecophotography, Marcy & Jerry Monkman
All photographs by the authors, unless otherwise noted.
Cover Design: Elisabeth Leydon Brady
Book and Map Design: Carol Bast Tyler

Distributed by The Globe Pequot Press, Inc.

Library of Congress Cataloging-in-Publication Data
Older, Julia, 1941–
        Nature walks in the New Hampshire lakes region / Julia
Older & Steve Sherman.
            p. cm.
        "An AMC nature walks book."
        Includes index.
        ISBN 1-878239-59-7 (alk. paper)
        1. Hiking—New Hampshire—Guidebooks. 2. Walking—
New Hampshire—Guidebooks. 3. Nature study—New
Hampshire—Guidebooks. 4. New Hampshire—Guidebooks. I.
Sherman, Steve, 1938– . II. Title.
GV199.42.N42O45   1997
796.51'09742—DC21   97-6637
                                                                        CIP

**Due to changes in conditions,
use of the information in this book
is at the sole risk of the user.**

Printed on recycled paper using soy-based inks.
Printed in the United States of America.

10 9 8 7 6 5 4 3 2   00 01 02

Contents

West

Introduction

Water covers one-sixteenth of the surface of New Hampshire. The Connecticut, Merrimack, Pemigewasset and Contoocook Rivers feed 43,000 miles of streams created by a huge watershed originating from the White Mountains to the north. Disastrous flooding in 1936 led to a series of dams along the Merrimack and these other rivers to protect Concord, Manchester, and points south in Massachusetts.

The king of lakes, Winnipesaukee, measures twenty-two miles long and ten miles wide and was formed millions of years ago when a soufflé-like crust of molten volcanic magma collapsed, leaving a ring dike, later filled by the water of the ice ages. Other large lakes in the Central Region include Newfound and Sunapee to the west and Ossipee, Wentworth, Winnisquam, and the "golden pond" of Squam to the east.

Dramatic waterfalls spill over precipices near abandoned mill sites, and flooded lakes seep into vast marshes. Specialized bogs with floating mats of vegetation twenty feet deep feature carnivorous pitcher plants and rare species of aquatic orchids and tundra flowers. The larger bodies of water give way to smaller glacier-formed kettle ponds, tray-size geological potholes, and clear bottles of New Hampshire spring water. Most of the natural wonders on these walks are related in some way to this unlimited ever present resource.

Locations

The walks selected for this guide are located north of Concord to the base of the White Mountains and west from the Connecticut River on the Vermont border to the eastern border of Maine.

Interstate 93 above Concord and below the White Mountains divides central New Hampshire into nearly equal sections. New Hampshire Route 25 has broad shoulders, is well paved, and offers access to many of the walks in the eastern Lakes Section. Interstate 89 from Concord speeds travelers to the northern part of the western Sunapee/Dartmouth Section.

On the west side of central New Hampshire the heavily wooded Monadnock/Sunapee Greenway (MSG) gives way to such high mountain peaks as Kearsarge and Cardigan and mature North Country forest. East of Interstate 93, the tidal estuaries of the Atlantic are replaced by freshwater lakes, and ponds and the Ossipee and Sandwich Mountain Ranges to the north.

Choosing a Walk

The fifty walks in this book include trails at nature centers, state parks and forests, undeveloped land tracts owned by the Society for the Protection of New Hampshire Forests (SPNHF), designated historic sites, urban parks, Audubon wildlife sanctuaries, U.S. Corps of Engineers Recreation Areas, and county and private preserves. Sample walks on three major long trails—the Monadnock-Sunapee Trail (50 miles), the Appalachian Trail (2,000 miles) and the state-long New Hampshire Heritage Trail (230 miles)—are included.

None of these walks is more than three miles round-trip; most are far less. We rated the majority of them easy to moderate with only a few being difficult. Of course, this depends on a walker's perspective. To us, easy means a flat, graded, well-marked trail without notable obstacles. Moderate describes a few sections of heavy breathing and some negotiable obstacles such as clambering over a few boulders or pussyfooting around a mudhole. Trail maintenance naturally factors into accessibility. A difficult trail might require extensive climbing, bushwhacking, or an infallible sense of direction.

We have focused on pleasant, short, day walks—not strenuous hikes. We've kept the selection diverse and family oriented since the Central Region is a popular vacation and recreation area. For example, grandparents might stroll the urban trail in Wolfeboro. High school and college students can check out a wilderness pond or walk a newly blazed section of the New Hampshire Heritage Trail. Lovers might find Paradise Point at Newfound Lake the perfect honeymoon spot. And those hiking with children can take them to see the animals at the Holderness Science Center. There's a walk for everyone in *Nature Walks in the New Hampshire Lakes Region*.

Walking (crawling, running, jumping, skipping) with Children

Holding the hand of a child and looking at the world of nature from a youngster's viewpoint can offer refreshing discoveries. Children are natural explorers and can point out many features that adults may miss or ignore. Children are closer to the ground than adults and may spot wild strawberries or a caterpillar.

But they also might put little objects of nature into their mouths. One way to avoid compulsive tasting is to equip children with small, sturdy plastic bags for them to carry discoveries home for examination later.

Keep in mind that children have shorter legs than adults and expend a lot of energy on exciting nature walks. To keep them going, bring along plenty of high-energy snacks such as raisins and cookies to eat during frequent rest stops.

Go slowly. Enjoy what they discover. Find them kid-size walking sticks. Be sure to hold their hands near water. A little information goes a long way with children, but bear in mind that these walks are in the woods, not a neighborhood park. Although children like to shout, try to teach them that if they're quiet they'll see more furry friends.

Walks that might be appropriate for children under eight years of age include:

East

- New Hampshire Farm Museum & Jones Forest; Jones Forest Trail

- Merrymeeting Lake New Hampshire Fish Hatchery; Powder Mill Fish Hatchery Ponds Trail

- Abenaki Tower Walk

- Castle Springs; Falls of Song Footpath and Trout Pond Trail

- Science Center of New Hampshire; Gephart Exhibit Trail (animals)

- Madison Boulder State Wayside; Boulder Trail

West

- Mount Kearsarge Indian Museum; Medicine Woods Path

- Philbrick-Cricenti Bog; all three trails

- Sanbornton I-93 Rest Area; Sanbornton Boulder Nature Trail

- Hannah Dustin Memorial Historic Site; Merrimack River Memorial Trail

- Profile Falls Recreation Area; Profile Falls Trail

- Paradise Point Audubon Nature Center; Elwell and Lakeside Trails

Fees and Seasons

Fees may be required for state parks and private environmental and wildlife agencies. Some historic sites charge for tours of the buildings but allow visitors to walk on the trails gratis. Fees are used to keep the trails well maintained and protected. For the few trails that require fees, costs are nominal and often a donation is asked instead. Fees are subject to change.

New Hampshire is a four-season state. Mud season is flood season, sometimes extending from March until mid-June. Snow may fall early and obstruct the trails, especially in the more northern areas. Although the New Hampshire autumn is spectacular, the crisp blue days of fall coincide with duck and deer hunting season from October into early December. When in doubt, find out. Call ahead.

What to Wear and How to Prepare

Feet first. Although these walks are casual, wear good boots. A trail is no place for bare feet and thin, flimsy footgear. Make sure you wear rubber soles and your ankles are supported.

Socks second. A long, wet winter leads to a long wood-tick season. (These are not the notorious microscopic deer ticks that carry Lyme disease.) The prevalent wood ticks thrive in long-stemmed grasses and are active into late spring. To help keep ticks from your body, wear long, thick Tyrolean-style socks and tuck pant legs into your socks and boots. Some walkers suggest wearing light-colored clothing to better see these insects the size of a capital O on this page. De-tick before getting into the car. Throw the ticks away. Then for home tick inspection, select a bathroom or uncarpeted room. Disrobe and carefully go over each item of clothing as well as all body parts. Pinch off ticks with a tissue. We once stomped on a tick four thunderous times and it merely crawled away unperturbed. The only sure way of ridding ticks from your life is to flush them down the toilet drain where they rightly belong.

If you spot a welt or rash on your skin or develop a fever that might be connected with an outing, definitely see a physician.

Some walkers wear shorts. The great majority of these walks are clear of brush, but a briar can scratch your thigh, you might unknowingly sit on poison ivy, a mosquito can land on your calf. The choice of shorts or long pants is yours. The same applies to short-sleeve shirts.

Hooded nylon windbreakers are versatile. They're light, mosquito-proof, handy during rain- or windstorms, and can be spread on the ground for sitting. If you become too warm, you can remove a windbreaker and tie it around your waist. The pockets are useful for carrying this book.

Bandannas come in handy also. They can be dipped into stream water to cool your face and neck, used to swab scraped skin, and worn on your neck or head to add protection from the sun.

Finally, if you don't like hats, be sure to take along a tube of sunscreen to protect your face.

Travel light and enjoy the walk. You aren't climbing Mount Everest. Carry the minimum. The following is our checklist:

- water

- lightweight, pocket-size nature identification guides for trees, mushrooms, wildflowers, ferns

- camera

- packets of hand tissues

- small pair of binoculars

- snacks or a gorp mix of raisins, almonds, and jelly beans

- knapsack if you're planning a picnic

- state road map for general directions

Walking and Gawking

The introduction to the Interstate 93 Sanbornton Boulder trailhead typifies what these walks are all about: "Our trail will lead you to natural happenings that put you in touch with the resources around you."

The walks aren't marathons, speed races, or power hikes. Go easy. Open up your senses. Enjoy the sights, sounds, colors, and textures.

Not to worry about getting lost. The large majority of the paths are so well worn that it's merely a matter of following "the yellow brick road." If a trail does have blazes and you come to a double blaze, this means a sharp change of direction or a junction lies ahead.

Any environment has more than one obvious central zone. Look up, look down. Examine life beneath the water surface, behind rocks and boulders —wildlife thrives everywhere. From tiny red-headed British soldiers lichen to huge oak trees, from delicate spring azure butterflies to strong-winged turkey vultures, the great outdoors teems with life. The pungency of sweet ferns, the fragrance of the pines, the lapping of shore water, the chirps and chatterings of chipmunks—all is alive and enlivens our senses.

On these outings everyday problems seem to slip away. We hope you experience moments of bliss and calm on these walks, as we have, and that they carry over after you return home, injecting a new awareness and refreshment into your everyday lives.

Acknowledgments

Many people offered their support for and interest in this book. They include Nancy Norwalk, director, Plainfield Public Library; Don Fitts, park guide, the Daniel Webster Birthplace; Cynthia Hunt, Canterbury Shaker Village; Nancy Beck, Science Center of New Hampshire; Thomas S. Curren, executive director, Lakes Region Conservation Trust; Maureen Marsh, assistant director, the Libby Museum; Daniel DeHart, forester, State Forest Nursery in Boscawen; Ralph and Rachel Pugh, the New Hampshire Farm Museum; Virginia Moulton and Joan DeBrine, Charleston Conservation Commission; Bob Fossett, director, and Theresa Michaels, fish culturalist, Powder Mill Fish Hatchery; Bud Thompson, director, Kearsarge Indian Museum. Our special thanks to Ola Frank for skillfully coordinating the project and to Carol Bast Tyler for her artful eye.

Locator Map

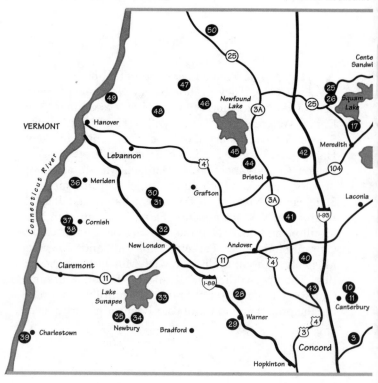

White Mountains

VERMONT

Connecticut River

Hanover

Lebanon

Meriden

Cornish

Claremont

Charlestown

Newbury

Bradford

Grafton

New London

Lake Sunapee

Warner

Hopkinton

Newfound Lake

Bristol

Andover

Concord

Meredith

Laconia

Squam Lake

Cente Sandwi

Canterbury

Southern New Hampshire

1. Bellamy River

2. Blue Job Mountain

3. Oak Hill Fire Tower

4. NH Farm Museum

5. Branch Hill Tree Farm

6. Cooper Cedar Woods

7. Weeks Woods

8. Mount Major State Forest

9. Powder Mills Fish Hatchery

10, 11. Shaker Village

12. Lang Pond Country Road

13. Knights Pond

14. Lake Wentworth State Beach

East

Bellamy River Audubon Wildlife Sanctuary
Border Trail (Loop)
Dover

- **1.2 miles**
- **1 hour**
- **easy**

This prime bank of tidal land along the mouth of the Bellamy River and a cove of Little Bay offers the best of salt- and freshwater ecosystems.

Lush fields make an inviting beginning. Start walking from the parking area with the woods on the left and a field fenced with wire to your right.

The Audubon Bellamy River Sanctuary sign marks the entrance at the end of the field boundary. Pick up a trail guide leaflet from the mailbox and enter the white pine woods. Watch your step; the pines have shallow root systems, and many of the roots surface in a knobby tangle on this trail.

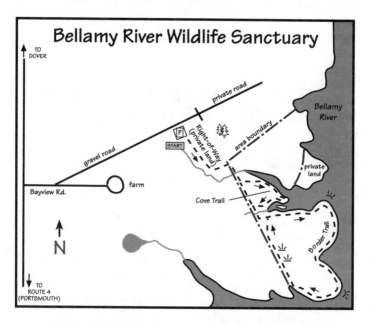

Bellamy River Wildlife Sanctuary

TO
DOVER

private road

Bellamy
River

P
START

Right-of-Way
(private land)

area boundary

gravel road

private
land

Bayview Rd.

farm

Cove Trail

N

Border Trail

TO
ROUTE 4
(PORTSMOUTH)

Cross a footbridge over a rivulet; oaks appear now. At 0.2 mile is a red metal blaze to the left indicating the Cove Loop Trail, which follows two prongs of a river inlet. Look straight ahead for the gold Border Trail blazes.

Here you'll find hardwoods uncrowded by undergrowth. In spring the leaf mulch provides enough moisture for a carpet of mayflowers dotted with their strangely speckled leaves, as well as the drooping bell of the yellow-flowered adder's tongue, purple and white wood violets, the five-petaled white wood anemone, and other wildflowers. We spotted several busy bumblebees collecting nectar from these delicate early spring bloomers.

At the junction of the Border Trail Loop (0.4 mile) bear left, keeping the river inlet to your left. Now the smell of the tidal flat and shoreline sedges is prominent. During summer these swampy inlets provide habitat for green-back and great blue herons, greater yellowlegs, and other waterfowl and shorebirds plying the oozy mud for frogs and small fish.

This peninsula juts into the confluence of the fresh-water Bellamy River and a cove off Little Bay, whose waters flow to and from the ocean via the tidal estuary of the Piscataqua River. Because of a rich daily ebb and flow of nutrients, the ten-mile-long estuary is a most hospitable environment for a wide variety of coastal plants and animals—one of the most varied of coastal ecosystems.

The Border Trail Loop affords sparkling water views. At the first outlook, unfortunately, the noise from Spaulding Turnpike across the inlet is inescapable.

Continue skirting the shore through an airy stand of white birch. At 0.8 mile the second outlook encompasses Royalls Cove to the right. An impressively tall shagbark hickory provides an ideal backrest (the peeling bark of the mature trunk makes it an easy tree to identify). Now follow the trail around the jut of land so the cove is to the left.

Here in the open sweep of the tidal basin all sorts of creatures populate the shore, including flotillas of horse-shoe crabs. Mature crabs shed their helmet-shaped shells. Like an invasion of amphibious tanks, they drag spiny tails across the ocean floor, while with their mouths they gobble from clam and oyster beds. Infuriated by these voracious armored creatures eating their

Yellow-flowered adder's tongues have mottled leaves and are smaller than trout lilies—both bloom in moist woodlands in the spring.

steamer specials, nineteenth-century coastal farmers plowed them into their fields for fertilizer. But horseshoe crabs are as prolific as ever. In fact, their primitive but durable structure has allowed them to survive more than 500 million years. Related to ancient sea scorpions, they are indeed "living fossils."

Each spring battalions of male horseshoe crabs cling to female life buoys, churning sperm over eggs tiny and abundant as grains of sand. The infant crabs settle down to seventeen winters buried in sand and mud waiting for the next phase of the cycle, when once more they shed their shells. Using compound eyes at the base of the spine and bristling mouths strategically centered between no fewer than twelve pairs of legs, they feed on

*Even without leaves, this shagbark hickory is easy to
identify.*

starfish, mussels, clams, and other tidbits unfortunate
enough to be in their way.

Pass through airy beech and other hardwood forest.
The Border Trail Loop ends in another tenth of a mile.
Follow gold blazes back. Cross the two footbridges (with
the field now on your left) to the parking area.

A word of comfort: sea breezes and salt air seem inhospitable to black flies in the spring (between May 7 and June 15), although you won't see as many water birds as you would between July and September.

Getting There

From Dover, drive on NH 108 south until the intersection with US 4. Head east on US 4 for about 4 miles. Turn left onto Back River Road and drive straight 0.8 mile. Turn right on Bayview Road. Drive 0.5 mile. Pass a sign for Declan Drive on the left near a stand of pines and bear left at the Y junction ahead onto a gravel road. Drive 0.2 mile to the Audubon sign and parking area on the right.

From Spaulding Turnpike, take Exit 6 west (toward Concord). Drive 0.8 mile and turn right on Back River Road. Drive another 0.8 mile straight. Turn right on Bayview Road. Drive 0.5 mile. Pass a sign for Declan Drive on the left near a stand of pines. Bear left at the Y junction ahead onto a gravel road and drive 0.2 mile to the Audubon sign and parking area on the right.

Affiliated Organizations

The Audubon Society of New Hampshire; 603-224-9909.

Blue Job Mountain

Blue Job Summit Trail
Strafford

- **1 mile**
- **45 minutes**
- **moderate**

A view-rich walk up a mountain topped with pines and a fire tower.

One of the unusual treats of this walk is the wide, southern, long-range view from only halfway to the summit. It's the kind of walk that requires you to turn around for the wonderful rolling hill scenes you'll miss if you keep trudging upward. Of course, you can see the scenes on the way down—but why not enjoy them twice?

The trailhead is located at a small parking lot opposite a house painted red when we were there. The lot is usually crowded since this is a popular spot. Two main trails take walkers to the 1,356-foot summit and fire tower. One begins between the boulders to the left of the parking area and proceeds directly up the mountain. The second trail, which we prefer, begins at the aluminum bar gate about thirty feet down the road to the left of the parking lot.

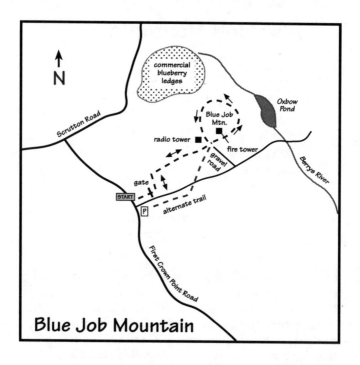

Blue Job Mountain

Pass around the gate and follow the well-trod trail as it turns to the left in about twenty-five feet. Signs and blazes are unnecessary; the wide, flat path at the outset is plain and simple.

Snow runoff spilling down the mountain and settling beside the footpath has provided ideal growing conditions for a small patch of cranberries in a moist area to the right of the trail. New England colonists called these tart fruit "crane berries." Eventually, the "e" was lost and—voila! Cranberries.

In about 300 feet pass through an opening in an old stone wall and follow the rocky trail up a slight incline.

A radio tower attached to the ledges stands below the forested summit to your right. In less than 100 feet a wide, eroded channel of earth on the right reveals a green maintenance building and a trail along the eroded wide rubble and stone tote road leading to it.

Continue your climb upward on the exposed runoff channel leading to the radio tower and building. It's a moderately steep fifty feet before the grade falls off. From this point to the radio tower, be sure to turn around now and then for long sweeping views of rolling hills across the entire southern horizon.

Turkey vultures, whose population is on the increase in the state, soar over Blue Job most of the summer. They're usually much too high to see their bright red heads. But they can be identified by their gliding flight and long wingspan. Black underwing feathers separate the turkey vulture from most birds of prey, which have distinct white or tan markings.

The trail disappears on the ledges. This section is open and grassy with scatterings of low, prickly juniper bushes and birch saplings. The aerial tower remains in sight; simply take the shortest pathway toward it.

As you approach the green cement-block building, the terrain steepens for about seventy-five feet. Head for the left side and, once you're behind the house, continue veering slightly to the left into the woods.

The trail to the fire tower at the summit now moves through pine-dominated woods. A large blue paint blotch on a tree behind and to the left of the building is a clue toward the mostly unblazed trail. Now, curve

Aspens, like birches, produce caterpillar-looking catkin flowers in spring.

around to the right and in about fifty feet the trail becomes more defined, drawing you into a completely different environment. This sudden change in terrain is one of the charms of Blue Job. The mature evergreens soften the light, cool the air, and silence your footsteps on the thick layer of needles.

About 200 feet into the woods on a short flat stretch, look for what is called a "whaleback." This humpback of granite ridge surfaces in the middle of the trail from the granite depths left over from the erosion of softer rock. The remainder of the walk includes a few steep inclines of exposed granite.

A half mile from the trailhead, the fire tower on the summit appears. The summit is wooded, but you can see sections of the horizon north toward the White Mountains, and from the top of the fire tower (if the fire lookout invites you) is a full-circle panorama.

Return by the same route or via the trail to the left of the fire tower steps. (This alternate trail moves through more-deciduous forest, which seems warmer and more buggy than the conifers.) However, both trails return you to the parking lot.

Getting There

From Rochester, drive two miles west on NH 202A (Main Street passes under U.S. 202) to First Crown Point Road. At a Y junction, take First Crown Point Road (202A veers left as a sign indicates) for 5.5 miles through ascending, rolling farmland. The parking area is on the right opposite a red house. (Although maps show that Blue Job Mountain can be approached from the west by NH 28 through North Barnstead, this route is not recommended.)

Oak Hill Fire Tower
Loudon

- **1 mile**
- **45 minutes**
- **moderate**

*A wooded footpath of gentle inclines past
large cellar holes to a steel fire tower.*

Especially enjoyable in early spring before the mud
flows and the trees leaf, the trail offers an appealing
openness. This makes a good family outing. Walk from
the Fire Tower/NH Forestry sign up the wide dirt Fire
Tower Road lined with many large oaks. These broad-
crowned white oak trees came to dominate the forest
here after an Asiatic blight killed most of the American
chestnuts in this area during the 1920s. The leaves of the
white oak have seven to eleven rounded lobes and are
reddish pink when they first appear in spring and when
they fall in autumn.

Black oaks also grow on Oak Hill. They have spiny-
tipped, pointed leaves and dark bark; their acorn caps
have a pronounced knob on the bottom. You'll see here
too that white pine seedlings are gradually taking over
the understory beneath the oak canopy.

In about 0.3 mile cross a small brook. In another 0.1
mile an impressive granite cellar hole comes into view

Oak Hill
Fire Tower

on the right side of the road. A local hiker remembers it
as a farmhouse with a poultry house and several out-
buildings; during the nineteenth century much of the
East Concord land was open pasture. Granite, an
igneous rock, fluctuates in color from the light gray
mammoth slabs cut for this Rock of Ages cellar to the
pink white outcrops seen elsewhere in the area.

Trailside granite is about as immovable as you can
get, but in early springtime look too for the intriguing,
slowly unfolding fiddlehead ferns scattered along the

way. Ferns favor edges of rivulets and brooks, but they also grow in moist soil that may not be obvious with high water content, especially under tree canopies away from the sun. These fern shoots appear as coils of fronds tucked into themselves. They emerge first as small, flat, half-dollar size fuzzy rounds on individual plant stems. Usually, you see several fiddleheads grouped at slightly different stages of unfurling toward their full length, which can extend to four and five feet, sometimes more.

Fiddleheads can be associated with many different fern shoots growing from the soil in spring, but in particular they are known mostly as young cinnamon ferns. Cinnamon ferns in full growth are widespread. Their fronds spread more than a foot wide and up to five feet

In spring, look for fiddlehead ferns along the trail.

long. Native Americans, especially in Maine, gathered fiddlehead ferns for food.

At 0.5 mile, the Fire Tower Road follows a short, steep rise and veers to the right. Keep on the easily followed trail making its way to the fire tower complex of small buildings.

On weekends the Fire Tower Road has a lot of foot traffic. Most families climb the mile (round-trip) to the tower. But unless the fire warden is on duty and invites you into the tower, be satisfied with ground-level views at the grown-in summit.

Later as a side stop, you might like to spend some time at the Turle Town Pond turnout nearby on Oak Hill Road. This offers some pleasant bird, plant, and wetlands watching.

Getting There

From I-93 north past Concord, take Exit 16. Make a very short diagonal jog left and drive straight uphill on Shawmut Road. At 0.7 mile veer left (at Oak Hill sign) onto Oak Hill Road. Pass Turtle Town Pond at 1.5 miles. Keep driving uphill. At 4.0 miles the Oak Hill Fire Tower sign is on the left side of the road. (A house with a four-story turret is on the right.) You may park on either side of the road. (Note: Disregard the mileage on the Fire Tower sign. The walk to the tower is a little more than one mile round-trip.)

Affiliated Organizations

The Concord Conservation Commission owns twenty-three acres of wetland on Turtle Town Pond, with a turnout and ramp for fishing and boating.

New Hampshire Farm Museum

Jones Forest Trail (Loop)

Milton

- **0.5 mile**
- **30 minutes**
- **easy**

A tree-identification trail beginning along an old cow path flanked by stone walls and circling through mixed woods.

Because the trail is part of the New Hampshire Farm Museum, this can be a doubly enjoyable outing. Open to the general public, the museum offers an historical look at the tools and times of an 1890 farmstead. The outsized barn is full of displays that demonstrate beekeeping; butter-and-cheese dairy techniques; and maple-sugar making, including a giant 1700s scalding kettle.

If you're lucky, you might have Rachel Pugh as a tour guide through the farmhouse itself. She's worked on a farm all her long life, was born one mile away, and comes from seven generations of family farmers in the area. She'll show you around the interior of the 1780 cape and the 1810 Levi Jones Tavern. These buildings (including the barn) are all connected, an example of how additions grew into a single large complex over the decades.

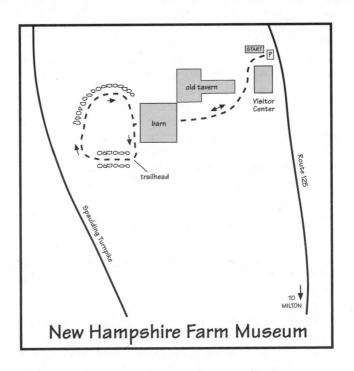

New Hampshire Farm Museum

(Scheduled throughout the summer and fall months at the museum are special days—Fiber to Fabric Day, Llama Day, Children's Day, Sale and Auction, Cribbage Pairs Tournament. Check the museum for exact events and days.)

We were fortunate, too, to have Rachel's son, Ralph Pugh, guide us on the identification trail in the woods behind the barn. You reach the trailhead by walking through the barn past the extraordinary collection of local milk bottles on exhibit. The trail begins about a hundred feet to the diagonal left of the rear entrance to the barn.

Scout Troop 155 cleared the trail and twenty identification markers are spaced around the loop. Walkers who are relatively new to the woods will find these especially informative in identifying some of the trees and plants that grow nearly everywhere in the state.

The first third of the trail leads straight down a path between two stone walls about twenty feet apart. "In the old days," Ralph said, "they drove cattle through here. That's why it's called a cow path."

Before moving on too far, look for a broad beech fern on the right close to the wall. This foot-high fern is named according to its broad-based pinna (the individual "leaf" of the blade). The fern grows in rich, moist woods, exactly where it should be on this trail.

Marker 2 identifies a red maple. You can identify this tree throughout the year by its persistent reddish tints (red buds in spring; reddish twigs; red veins in the summery green leaves; and, most notable of all, its fiery red fall leaves).

A hefty, short-needled eastern hemlock marks where the trail turns to the right from the cow path near a marked old dump site (these woods, after all, were once cleared for a working farm). Then comes a white pine, with its five long needles to a cluster, and a striped maple (also known as moosewood), which has a thin green trunk of vertical white stripes.

Ralph pointed out at markers 11 and 12 what is called on this trail the "Centurion," a giant oak, and an outsized "bull" pine.

The trail curves at a shallow angle to the right on flat terrain until it heads straight for about a hundred feet along another stone wall. At this vantage point, markers 13 and 14 show an interesting juxtaposition of forests.

On the right of the wall, you'll notice a tree farm of red (or Norway) pines standing straight and tall in neat, planted rows. On the left side of the wall (which is owned by the Society for the Protection of New Hampshire Forests) grows a natural mixed woods of maple, oak, beech, white pine, birch, and other wild trees, a sight that shows the striking difference between the two extremes of woodlot usage.

This trail also identifies several flowering plants along the way, including the lady-slipper, a prolific wild

Many generations have worked the Jones Farm land for more than two centuries.

orchid that grows well in moist northern woods. The foot-shaped fuchsia flowers dangle from sturdy stalks. Please don't dig up these orchids; they are extremely difficult to transplant, so you would merely end up killing these yearly bloomers. It is also illegal.

Farther on, the trail passes by good examples of spruce, American elm, and an apple tree growing in competition like a long-necked giraffe to reach the sunlight.

Keep your eyes on the ground, too. Marker 19 identifies poison ivy near a jack-in-the-pulpit. Note its characteristic light green protective hood; it hides the secretive "Jack" stalk of the flower. The bulb of this intriguing plant once was referred to as Indian turnip.

The trail returns to the rear of the barn through an opening at the edge of the woods close to the stone wall and cow path.

Getting There

From Rochester on the Spaulding Turnpike, drive northeast to Exit 18. Turn south on NH 125 and drive 1.4 miles to Jones Farm Museum on the right (a prominent sign indicates the museum). Park in the allotted space.

Other Information

New Hampshire Farm Museum
Route 125
Plummer's Ridge/P.O. Box 644
Milton, NH 03850
603-652-7840

Open May through November. Groups welcome. Fee charged.

Branch Hill Tree Farm

Tree Farm Road
Milton

- **1.2 miles**
- **45 minutes**
- **easy**

A two-part walk, first through a tree farm of Norway (red) pines, then on a wide woodland lane past a cool forest brook.

If you walk through the tree farm at Branch Hill (one of 1,700 in the state) before entering the wild forest, you'll appreciate the startling difference between man-made and natural woodland. Carl Siemon's Branch Hill Tree Farm, managed by his daughter, Cindy Wyatt, is a three-time winner of the New Hampshire Outstanding Tree Farm of the Year award (1976, 1982, and 1991). The sponsors of the national program in the state are the Society for the Protection of New Hampshire Forests, New Hampshire Timberland Owners Association, and the University of New Hampshire Cooperative Extension Service.

    Pass to the side of the white metal gate. A sign reads: "Landowners providing public access reminds walkers that this is private property opened for your walking enjoyment, not for vehicular traffic, hunting, or careless visitors."

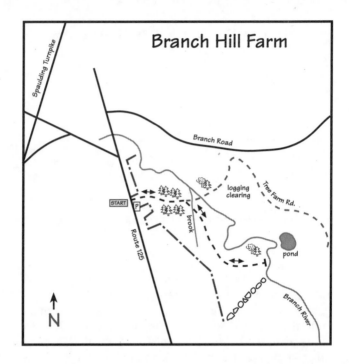

Branch Hill Farm

In about ninety feet a double-rutted sand road lined with tall white pines turns into an extensive red pine tree farm.

At this stage of their growth (about twenty feet high) these softwood, long-needled trees are still bushy and cone shaped, and have boughs low to the ground. (Mature *Pinus resinosa* often peak at eighty-five feet.) The bark is tinged red, and later in the growth the trunk grows in characteristic shieldlike sections and becomes a more pronounced rust color.

Also called Norway pine (not to be confused with

Norway spruce), this species adapts well to well-drained soils like the sand you're walking on. Fast-growing red pine is widely used for the reforestation of gravel pits and clearcut logging sites. It also is cultivated and farmed for telephone and utility poles.

The ecozone beneath these trees hosts a microhabitat of lichen with red reproductive structures on top. Named "British soldiers" by colonists, they tint the understory with pools of blood red color. Parasol mushrooms also proliferate in the ruts of the road and the shade of the pine boughs.

After 0.25 mile under the open sky, the road, which isn't blazed, continues up a slight incline and into the mixed forest. Right away you cross a brook and enter the quiet of hemlocks and thick black-trunked white pines. This upland forest is far enough from blacktop highways

Tree farms supply red (Norway) and pitch pines to utility and fencing companies, and provide plantings for reforestation.

to lend a relaxing away-from-it-all saunter to your gait.

At 0.4 mile a short side path to the left leads thirty feet down to a series of woodland pools fed by another brook. Towhees, wood thrushes, nuthatches, chickadees, and the noisier voices of crows and hawks punctuate the vernal bliss of this wetland. Alarmed frogs croak and leap from decayed logs. Deer browse down to drink in the cooler hours of the day (we saw many two-prong, long and oval deer-hoof tracks etched into the soft soil).

Return to the tote road, turn left, and resume the walk. At 0.5 mile another brook passes beneath the road. Beech, white pine, and birch crowd the edges of an extensive backwater downhill to the left paralleling the road.

A wide logging stage at 0.6 mile abruptly ends easy access to the property. Unsightly ruts from skidders and other machinery, stumps, and logging litter clutter the landscape here. We suggest you head back.

Return with the brook backwater to your right now, gradually coming down Branch Hill Tree Farm through the red pines to your car at the gate.

Getting There

On the Spaulding Turnpike north from Rochester, take Exit 18. Turn south on NH 125 toward Milton and the Jones Farm Museum. Drive 0.6 mile and park on the left of the road at the white gate marked Branch Hill Farm. The gate also has a sign reading Wildlife Stewardship Area and Tree Farm.

Other Information

The New Hampshire Farm Museum is just down the road, and Cooper Cedar Woods is in the vicinity.

Cooper Cedar Woods
Cooper Cedar Woods Trail (Loop)
New Durham

- **0.9 mile**
- **30 minutes**
- **easy**

A varied walk past a heath bog and a prized mature grove of Atlantic white cedar protected by the SPNHF.

In the parking area of a cleared field at Cooper Cedar Woods, you'll notice how porous the soil is. These well-drained, nutrient-rich soil deposits of Ice Age glaciers provide habitat for white pine, hemlock, white and red oak, and in this particular upland woods, some glossy yew shrubs.

Follow the needled woodland path behind the large Cooper Cedar Woods sign to the loop turnoff at 0.1 mile. Here, at a small sign marked Trail, pick up a leaflet from the Society for the Protection of New Hampshire Forests (SPNHF) guide box. This guide includes a map of the loop by a heath bog, cedar swamp, esker, and an old swamp.

In May and June balls of wild sarsaparilla flowers bloom. Their clusters of three (looking like dandelions gone to seed) are quite profuse in the undergrowth. They are related to ginseng plants, which have yellow flowers

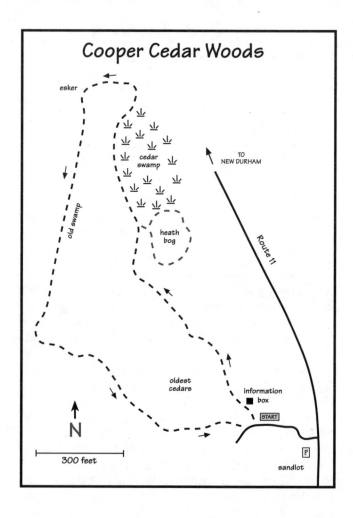

Cooper Cedar Woods

esker

cedar
swamp

old swamp

heath
bog

TO
NEW DURHAM

Route 11

oldest
cedars

information
box

START

N

300 feet

P

sandlot

blooming singly in July and August. The roots of both plants are cultivated by many cultures—ginseng as a cure-all and sarsaparilla as a root beer–type flavoring.

Unfortunately, in spring you probably won't want to linger for long to examine much of anything. The mosquitoes on this property are hungry and fierce. The SPNHF leaflet advises walkers that "insect repellent helps in summer, but poison ivy is rare." In other words, you won't have to worry about mosquito bites and a rash at the same time.

But though the shoulder-high magenta sheep-laurel blossoms in the heath bog are exquisite in spring, we suggest you take the walk during August or in the fall, when the sphagnum bog and cedar swamp are drier, friendlier, and not abuzz.

Deer browse these woods. We saw many deep hoof prints in the impressionable wet duff of the forest floor, and if you visit the woods at dawn or twilight you may catch a glimpse of them.

Climb the glacial esker at 0.4 mile. This low-lying but distinct ridge was formed of sand and gravel deposits carried by a stream of running water tunneling through the sheets of a glacier. Native Abenaki once walked on sinuous eskers in the coastal region because they provided high, dry ground and a good view.

Today, unfortunately, the end of the ridge overlooks a tract of land that has been clearcut by loggers. This barren area lies outside the protection of the SPNHF, striking evidence of the dichotomy between honoring and destroying the land. The mature stand of Atlantic white cedar that dominates Cooper Cedar Woods today at one

The hobblebush, a viburnum, reroots in early spring in a tangle of branch rhizomes, but by May it resembles its other name—bridalwreath.

time encompassed more than these remaining thirty acres.

At 0.6 mile is a considerable grove of the tall cedar trees. The flat sprays of blue-green needles cast a cool-toned shadow over the trail. The Atlantic white cedar, unlike the eastern red cedar, which is a juniper, is related to the Pacific red cedar, a giant conifer of the West Coast. The cones are small and the cedars prefer moist, boggy soil. Insects proliferate in cedar swamps, and pitcher plants and carnivorous flytraps take advantage of this easy prey. There is a swamp nearby, but the soil has built up beneath this mature grove of trees. The tall, straight trunks tower 80–150 feet high, and are rare because most of them were cut for timber long ago.

Seventeenth-century nature chronicler John Josselyn wrote, "This tree the English saw into boards to floor their rooms." The wood endures so well that New England fences, floors, roof shakes, and even church organs were made out of the Atlantic white cedar. The SPNHF hopes to maintain and regenerate this prized tree; the walker's awareness is a good beginning.

At 0.8 mile, after winding through the quieter isolation of the cedar forest, the loop ends. Walk the 0.1 mile on the same path back to the parking area.

Getting There

From NH 11 at the flashing red light at the junction with Depot Road to New Durham, drive 0.7 mile south toward Rochester. Pull off to the right of NH 11 and park at the Cooper Cedar Woods and Tree Farm signs.

From Spaulding Turnpike at Rochester drive 11 miles on NH 11 north. Pull off to the left at the Cooper Cedar Woods and Tree Farm signs.

Affiliated Organizations

The Society for the Protection of New Hampshire Forests
54 Portsmouth Street
Concord, NH 03301
603-224-9945

Weeks Woods (SPNHF)

Weeks Woods Trail (Loop)

Gilford

- **1.75 miles**
- **1 hour**
- **moderate**

This forested trail opens at the crest of an upland meadow onto a surprise view of Belknap Mountain.

A gradual ascent from the roadside through woods on tote roads takes you to a rewarding hillside overlook. From the town offices (see *Getting There* below), cross Rte. 11A and pass to the left of an upright millstone in memory of Robert Bruce Weeks. The Weeks family deeded this eighty-five-acre farm property to the Society for the Protection of New Hampshire Forests (SPNHF) in their son's honor.

Behind the entrance gate, walk uphill on a pleasant wide tote road. Walkers must keep in mind that this is a busy multiuse path. The trail is open to joggers and loggers, trail bikers, horseback riders, and cross-country skiers.

Good examples of "pasture" pines grow along the tote road. Pasture pines are left over from a time when sheep and cows grazed on this upland farm. The branches of seedlings torn and split by the flocks and herds establish separate trunks, making each pine resemble a

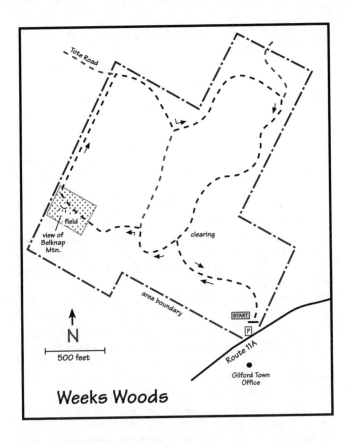

Weeks Woods

pitchfork stuck in the ground. A section of a felled pine trunk beside the trail exhibits at close hand the massive girth of these trees.

In about three-hundred yards, mixed woods of black oak and white birch give way to a handsome cluster of straight white pine deeper in the forest. These prime trees are selected by loggers over the pasture pines for their straight trunks, better growth, and easier access with a saw. The SPNHF actively promotes "wise forest management," and a flier (which may be picked up at the Gilford Town Library) informs visitors that "Weeks Woods continues to produce forest products." To our taste, though, logging litter, ruts left by heavy machinery, cleared patches of forest, and the sound of the chain saw aren't altogether in keeping with a peaceful woodland stroll.

At 0.2 mile you come to an oval clearing where hawkweed (yellow dandelion-like flowers on stalks a few feet high), black-eyed Susans, and purple-flowered vetch (trailing through the grass on vines) proliferate.

Turn left off the tote road and onto a wooded trail. At the next junction turn left again. (A narrow path continues straight.) Pass through a mucky area of sedge and tall cinnamon ferns.

Now walk uphill on hardscrabble (rock litter and earth) through a hemlock stand. Loggers leave the hemlock, which isn't of commercial timber value but is invaluable to deer as a shelter during winter snowstorms.

At 0.5 mile you come to the edge of a lush upland meadow overgrown with daisies, Queen Anne's lace, and thick-stalked, tall blue-green milkweed.

The summer pink florets of these broad-bloomed weeds transform into the familiar silky seed pods of fall. In the spring, milkweed plants especially attract the caterpillars of monarch and queen butterflies of the *Danaidae* family. Milkweed contains toxins which the caterpillars safely ingest and accumulate. After the butterflies break out of the chrysalids, these toxins continue to be stored in the wings and abdomen and detract predators.

The Weeks Woods does not extend past the opening in a stone wall at the top of the sloping meadow. Turn right and skirt the high upper western edge of the field. From the far corner, look back across the meadow to the horizon. A surprise view of Rowe Mountain (with the fire tower) and Belknap Mountain (2,384 feet) opens up, showcasing the dramatic topography of this region.

The trail is easy to this point. If you have toddlers or are an inexperienced walker, we suggest retracing your steps; continuing the loop through the logging area and back takes a bit of a scramble.

Clamber over the stone wall at the upper west corner and onto a narrow path blazed in red. At 0.7 mile climb across a second stone wall. Stones and tree litter give way to a pine-needle path. Walk downhill, bushwhacking

A beautiful millstone marks the entrance to Weeks Woods.

through a swampy muddy path lined with sensitive fern (scalloped chartreuse fronds) and ebony spleenworts (symmetrical oval pinnae on low-lying fronds about a foot long).

A stand of white birch precedes the 0.8-mile exit from the forest onto a logging road. Turn right and follow orange dot blazes through another deer yard of hemlocks identified by their short needles and swooping, dark green overhead boughs.

At the next junction turn left, still following the orange dot blazes downhill. At 1.2 miles pass through another swampy area with a drainage pipe laid across the trail.

At 1.3 miles another path comes in from the left. Turn right. A long, fairly flat section closes the loop at 1.5 miles. You will recognize the oval clearing from the beginning of your walk. Bear slightly left and proceed 0.2 mile back to the millstone and trail gate.

Getting There

From the junction of US 3 with NH 11, turn onto 11 east and drive 2.6 miles. Park at Gilford town offices on the right. Weeks Woods is opposite the Public Works Department and town offices on the north side of the road.

Affiliated Organizations

SPNHF
54 Portsmouth Street
Concord, NH 03301
603-224-9945

Nearby are Gunstock Recreation Area and Belknap Mountain.

Mount Major State Forest
Mount Major Summit Trail (Loop)
Alton

- **2.5 miles**
- **2 hours**
- **difficult** (boots recommended; not advisable for children under nine)

An often arduous, heart-pumping climb leads to top-of-the-world views of Lake Winnipesaukee and Alton Bay.

A sign at the beginning of the trail to Mount Major warns hikers to wear boots—and this is good advice. The trail seems harmless enough at the outset, but the soil is crumbly and at the top rocks litter the path.

Bring enough water and a snack. This is an energetic albeit energizing climb. And a word of caution: At times this is a strenuous climb. We saw several flushed and weepy children. This isn't a good mountain for small legs. The same goes for dogs. German shepherds, corgies, collies, Labs, golden retrievers, bloodhounds, mongrels—the mountain looked like a dog show. Canines may be man's best friend, but they scare off wildlife and leave unpleasant messages for hikers on the trail.

The trailhead is clearly visible at the end of the parking lot. At once you'll notice the trail gets heavy use, and

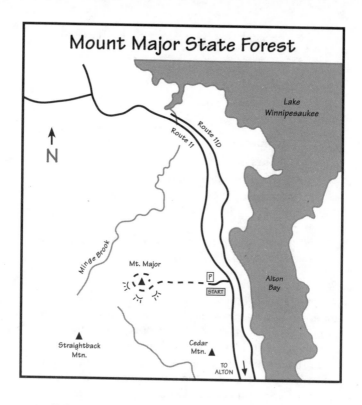

Mount Major State Forest

Lake Winnipesaukee

Route 11

Route 11D

N

Minge Brook

Mt. Major

P

START

Alton Bay

Straightback Mtn.

Cedar Mtn.

TO ALTON

runoff from spring snowmelt hasn't helped the overall erosion situation. Mount Kearsarge in Rollins State Park to the west and Grand Monadnock in Monadnock State Park to the south have confronted this problem in a variety of ways. Hefty logs placed in downward Vs every few yards catch the dirt and mud and build up this soil. Narrow drainage ditches dug horizontally across the trail also can direct runoff into the woods. This makes the going easier for hikers and preserves the mountain trail.

After a few hundred yards the climb is steeper. Pacing yourself early helps. The royal blue blazes are faint.

At 0.3 mile pass through a stone-wall opening. Like many mountains in New Hampshire, Mount Major once pastured sheep and cattle. The trail levels out at 0.5 mile and another stone wall appears on the right near a white "pasture" pine. Like the stone walls, this multi-trunked tree is evidence that the wood was once pasture. Years ago, when the pine was young, the lower branches were chewed and split off by grazing herds. The split tree branches drooped to the ground, rooted, and so formed three or four separate trunks at the base.

Enjoy this graded level section through sparse saplings. Notice the inordinate number of green-trunked trees with green-and-white striped trunks and broad, rounded goose-foot–shaped leaves. Commonly they are known, in fact, as goose-foot maples—or moosewood, since deer and moose find them just the right height for browsing.

At a blue arrow on a black-trunked sweet birch tree, turn left. The smooth, satiny bark of birches tempts trail crews to paint blazes on them. But birch wood is soft and short lived; walkers often must look for the blaze on a decayed or fallen trunk.

Start climbing again. Now you're on a stony spillway. At 0.7 mile note the barkless snag (a standing dead mammoth tree trunk—probably a white pine) riddled with woodpecker holes. You might hear the Woody Woodpecker laughter of the largest member of this family in the New Hampshire woods, the black-and-white-bodied, red-crested pileated woodpecker. (The other woodpeckers aren't pileated or crested.) Next in size is the white-chested, black-and-white-winged hairy woodpecker, which usually gives a loud warning chirp before flying in to land. The smallest is the downy woodpecker (a smaller version of hairy). Flickers and the small yellow-bellied sapsuckers look quite different, but they also belong to this family. They rarely winter over.

Just beyond, another snag provides a feeding station for insect-eating birds and shelter for such furry forest creatures as red squirrels and chipmunks.

At 0.8 mile a boulder field appears, and by 0.9 mile red Norway pines tower above, lending an alpine feeling to the climb.

By 0.95 mile the angle turns steep and you're walking on a trail of bedrock. Although Mount Major is only 1,784 feet high, the trees here are dwarfed by the harsh New Hampshire weather coming in across Lake Winnipesaukee from the White Mountains and Canada beyond.

At 1.0 mile the climb gets even steeper. A handrail would be welcome at this juncture. Be careful! A few pointers on mountain climbing: You can make your own switchbacks by zigzagging from one side of the trail to the other. Avoid stepping between sharp rocks; this is a good way to wrench an ankle. Flat rock is preferable to crumbly sand or soil. Stay at the edge of the trail, where you can safely grab a bush or sapling if you feel yourself slipping. Look down, but also ahead a few yards, mentally planning the best footing.

Just when you think you've reached the summit, you face a nearly vertical ascent. The going gets tough. Help each other.

By 1.2 miles all paths lead to the top. Choose the path of least resistance. The foundation of an old stone shelter marks the summit of Mount Major, but most people stop wherever they come out, relaxing on the open ledges to admire the glorious views.

To the east lies the long finger of Alton Bay, and directly to the north is the blue of Lake Winnipesaukee, encircling the forested and hilly Rattlesnake Island. Much closer below, in Mount Major State Forest, Minge Brook seeps into a large visible marsh. With binoculars, this is an ideal habitat to spot moose. Behind Straightback Mountain (1,887 feet) to the southwest is Belknap Mountain State Forest and another mountain with spectacular views, Belknap Mountain (2,384 feet).

From this vantage you can make out an unusual feature of New Hampshire geology. During the Mesozoic Era some 200 million to 100 million years ago, volcanic activity buried New Hampshire a mile deep in lava and ash. The earth's crust cooled and collapsed, caving in like the center of a soufflé, leaving a ring of crevices through which the molten magma from below bubbled and hardened into igneous rock. The Ossipee Mountains to the north of Lake Winnipesaukee form one of several circular "ring" dikes in New Hampshire. In fact, the state is known for having more ring dikes than any other area in the Western Hemisphere.

On this summit you will find marmolite, also known as serpentine. This magnesium silicate usually has a green hue, but the marmolite found by Edward Libby on

A steep climb to the summit of Mount Major results in rewarding views of Lake Winnipesaukee and Alton Bay.

this mountain and displayed in the Libby Museum (see the Lang Pond Road Walk on page 66) is yellow. Magnesium silicate in its fibrous state is mined commercially as asbestos.

Different grades of granite are mined in the Granite State. The granite in this region is a soft composite of quartz, feldspar, and mica. This friable black-and-white granite (pegmatite) breaks down and is mined for these substances. More-durable granite used in construction is found in the southwestern part of the state.

Blueberries and mountain cranberries poke from many rock crevices, glistening in the sun. Unlike bog cranberries that grow in water, the mountain berries are dwarfed, hugging damp rock crevices. They are edible, though extremely tart and best left to the birds. (Any plant you cannot absolutely identify should not be touched or eaten.)

Retrace your steps down the mountain. To the left of the main trail, we discovered a narrow, worn footpath in the woods that bypassed the arduous upper reaches on the main trail through a series of switchbacks. If you have a good sense of direction, you might come upon a similar detour that eliminates the steep section at the top.

Getting There

From the junction of NH 28A and NH 11 in Alton Bay, drive on NH 11 west for 4.1 miles. Turn left into the Mount Major parking lot at the prominent road sign to Mount Major. (The lot is often full during July and August weekends; parking overflows to the highway.)

Powder Mill Fish Hatchery

Powder Mill Trout Ponds Trail

Alton

- **0.8 mile**
- **45 minutes**
- **easy**

Fish graduate from fingerlings to lunkers in the raceways and ponds laid out along the spillway of Merrymeeting Lake.

Children especially will like this educational self-guided tour where they can learn how fish are raised. At the information shed near the parking lot, pick up a hatchery brochure which outlines the process involved in rearing and stocking trout in New Hampshire lakes and streams.

Cross the parking area from the shed to a boardwalk along the cement raceways; prominent signs designate the species of trout and salmon being raised. These concrete raceways are netted to prohibit kingfishers, herons, and other piscivorous birds from swooping into them for a free lunch. You'll also notice large yellow balloons with facelike patterns swinging from tall poles. They lend a festive atmosphere to the hatchery, although their practical function is to keep predatory birds away.

Turn right at a central asphalt walkway between two sets of raceways. The trout we saw had grown from

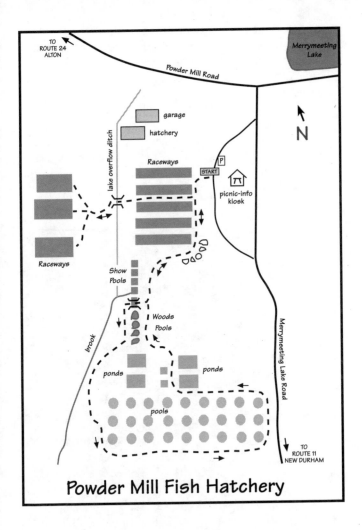

Powder Mill Fish Hatchery

spring fingerlings of two to three inches to seven-inch adults. A resident fish culturalist, Theresa Michaels, is constantly on the move with a feed bucket, feeding the larger fish three to four times a day, depending on the species. One hot August afternoon she explained that the rainbow trout were doing much better with the intense heat than the brown trout, which had schooled in one spot and weren't moving much. (Powder Mill Hatchery is open and operates all winter. The flowing icy water doesn't freeze and these trout seem to prefer it to the summer heat.)

Fish culturalist Theresa Michaels feeds the trout three to four times a day.

Water constantly circulates in the raceways where the trout are raised.

Proceed over a cement walkway that bridges a drainage ditch connecting Merrymeeting Lake above the hatchery with the fish ponds below. This channeled water eventually hooks up with a brook.

Turn left and maneuver around the hatchery building on the other side of the bridge.

Retrace your steps over the bridge to the boardwalk fronting the raceways. Turn right. Pass a stone wall and embankment on the left. A lone white pine offers welcome shade. (The raceways and pools deliberately are in the open so that foliage and evergreen needles and cones don't litter the water and add to the arduous task of cleaning them.)

This site has been in continuous use for almost 150 years. The first foundations erected in the early 1800s supported saw and grain mills. From 1857 through the early 1860s the mills were converted to meet a growing demand for blasting powder as the Civil War loomed large, then broke out. Production expanded until twenty-five tons of the volatile powder inadvertently exploded, destroying much of the mill. A second explosion halted production in 1863. This hatchery, built in 1947, represents a more benign use of the water-power system at Merrymeeting Lake.

On the right at 0.2 mile are a few separate pools in a grassy area. For a quarter a feeding machine releases a handful of fish-food pellets so visitors can feed the show trout in these pools. As we peered at the two-foot rosy-gold rainbow trout lazing in the shoals, we decided they could use a little weight watching and moved on.

Climb a ramp in plain sight to a footbridge to the left of the show trout pools and cross the stone-lined canal ditch, part of the early mill system. Turn left and descend a flight of stone steps with a handrail.

A tree-lined path extends the length of the ditch to the first of four wooded pools. Hemlock, red oak, and golden birch are far enough from the water so they don't interfere with the long, narrow pools, which are connected to each other by spillways. Debris is strained from the water through screen traps, and the water is kept oxygenated through a series of stepped spillways. The pools also are protected with nets and fencing because airborne predators as well as otter, muskrat, fisher, and other creatures are attracted to their rich store of fish.

At 0.3 mile the trail meets a dirt road that encircles a large open area. Wind around to the right on the road,

Water from Merrymeeting Lake is directed through this canal to a series of natural ponds where the larger trout continue to develop.

which parallels an overgrown natural brook that hosts families of wild ducks, song birds, mink, otter, and numerous water-loving plants.

The salmon are hatched and raised to yearling size 6–7 inches) on site here, but 2–3 inch brook, rainbow, and brown trout fingerlings are transferred to Powder Mill and raised for one year. To begin the salmon process landlocked salmon (a member of the trout family), are netted in Lake Winnipesaukee. The bellies of the females are stroked and 40,000–80,000 eggs collected. They are fertilized by milt sperm from the males and incubated in stacked trays and indoor holding tanks.

To the left at 0.4 mile are four open ponds grown in with reeds and some aquatic plants. We saw no schools of fish in these pools, which come closest to the natural habitat these cultivated fish will encounter.

Often while snorkeling in New Hampshire lakes, we've seen trout in their natural habitat, doing what comes naturally. With their bellies and heads, the fish form circular nests in gravel or sand on the lake bed. These plate-sized depressions are called "redds." The trout remove larger pebbles with their mouths, spitting the sand and pebbles outside the redd. They patiently float over them, guarding the deposited and fertilized eggs, which hatch in about five months.

Just beyond on the left you will come to three rows of circular cement pools with nine pools in each row. At 0.5 mile turn left and in a few yards more turn left again, so that you have walked completely around the circular ponds. Then turn right and walk between the natural ponds with two on each side. An entrance from Merrymeeting Road to this section of the hatchery comes in on the right where a dirt parking lot is located.

Head north at 0.6 mile, and when you reach the first of the woods pools, veer right onto an old tote road forming a high embankment on the opposite side of the pools. This mill road paralleled the earlier canal ditch and closes the loop part of your walk, ending at the earthen dam and footbridge. Return the way you came (show-fish pools and raceways now to the left).

Getting There

From the traffic rotary at Alton take NH 28 north. Drive 0.8 mile to Old Wolfeboro Road. Turn right and drive 1.9 miles to Powder Mill Road. Turn right and drive 2.4 miles. The hatchery is on the right after 0.1 mile, diagonally opposite the spillway of Merrymeeting Lake.

Other Information

Open 8:00 A.M. to 4:00 P.M. daily. For further information call 603-859-2041.

Canterbury Shaker Village

Turning Mill Pond Identification Trail (Loop)

Canterbury

- **1 mile**
- **1 hour and 15 minutes**
- **easy**

The trail follows the shoreline of
two Shaker-made ponds in a system of eight
—one quite isolated,
the other close to the hilltop village.

Founded in 1747 in England, the Shaking Quakers, or Shakers (so called for the trembling brought on by religious emotion), arrived in New York in 1774. Half a century later they had established eighteen communities in America. Canterbury Shaker Village was one of them.

To get to the trail, walk to the left and behind the main buildings fronting the road, where the gardens are located. A sign reading Trails and Gardens directs visitors down a mowed, sloping swath of lawn and past raised rose and herb beds. Near these herb gardens is a mailbox with guides to the Turning Mill Pond Identification Trail. (You may also pick up a flier at the brick administration building and visitor center near the parking lot.)

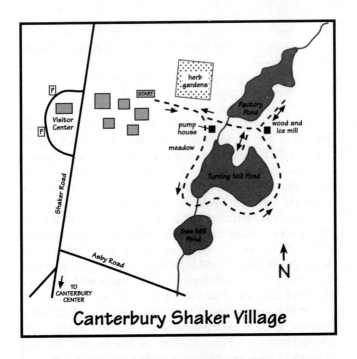

Canterbury Shaker Village

Turning Mill Pond is visible here from the hilltop. Turn right between two granite entry posts into the meadow and walk downhill parallel to a stone wall on the left. In the productive 1850s this village housed more than three hundred people by family groups: Church, North, West, and Second Families.

Turning Mill Pond was in use from 1818 to 1916, forming the mainstay of an elaborate system of "ditched" ponds for water power. At the foot of the hill is the old pump house road. (The granite pump house was being reconstructed, as were many of the buildings, when we were there.) The road to the left leads to a cross-country ski and snowmobile trail through Gilmanton to Laconia.

Facing the pump house, turn right onto a mowed path around the pond.

On your left is a tall honey locust tree with oval leaves on long fronds and prominent thorns on its branches. For a closer look examine the honey locust sapling that sways over the trail. The seemingly harmless fronds are armored with sharp thorns at the base, so be careful if you must push it out of the way. As the tree grows to maturity, these thorns also stud the trunk.

The first identification post on the trail is to the left and marks a butternut tree. The butternut is a white walnut with eleven to twelve opposing oval leaflets and long, green-husked edible nuts. English walnuts grown commercially are a different variety. Black walnuts have thicker hulls, dark bark, and a more earthy flavor.

White birch grow around the pond. At one time the women made Shaker boxes using prepared poplar from the Sabbath Day Pond Shakers in Maine. But with the advent of new machinery invented in 1806 by men in Chester, New Hampshire, they decided to be completely self-sufficient. According to Canterbury archives they "converted five poplar trees into the split and cured product, ready for weaving" into baskets that were sold in great quantity from 1843 on. Birch and poplar look somewhat alike, but poplar has rounder leaves and the bark looks like other trees at the bottom, with horizontal birchlike markings at the top as it matures. Poplar also is known as quaking aspen.

Sugar maple is identified here, too. It was tapped and the syrup used in the kitchen.

The flowers and berries in the meadow above the pond no doubt also were collected for their healing properties and used in the infirmary and kitchen.

Apart from its utilitarian purposes, this flowery meadow is a visual wonder. Tansy (flat, bright yellow flower clusters), blueberries (low bushes with small white flowers), loosestrife (tall, handsome magenta-flowered stalks), meadowsweet (a shrub of the *Spirea* genus with pinkish white blooms), pert black-eyed Susans—all color the tall nodding grasses.

Near the new pump house at 0.3 mile is a black cherry tree (marker 4), and beyond, near the new cement dam on Turning Mill Pond, elderberries crop up in great profusion.

Turn around to look behind markers 5 and 6. The remains of the 1817 old stone dam and ditch are visible in the weeds to the right above Saw Mill Pond. A few red cedar grow here among more elderberries, called common elder in the flier. The wide-topped clusters with small purple berries make sensational jelly, and no doubt the Shakers used them. But these American elders, we understand, can infect elms with disease.

This pond is extremely quiet and peaceful. At 0.4 mile a flat boulder invites walkers to sit in the shade of a lone white pine. Looking back where you've been, a beaver lodge that was hidden by the dam comes into view.

At 0.5 mile turn left and enter the woods through an opening in the stone wall. Marker 10 identifies a stand of soft, short-needled balsam fir, rock ferns (small ferns

Shaker Village from Turning Mill Pond.

growing from rock crevices), and the Canada mayflower (with two to three shiny, large spatulate leaves).

On the northeast side of the pond is a stone-lined spillway to Ingalls Dam, which directs flood water from the mills to the Soucook River. Here at the edge of Turning Mill Pond on the left is a rectangular stone engraved with a Greek cross, nothing more. One would guess it to be a gravestone, but the Shakers observed communal burial, with one memorial stone serving for the entire community. So the provenance of this stone remains a mystery.

If you brought your camera, this north end of Turning Mill Pond provides a picturesque view of the Shaker buildings on the hilltop.

At 0.6 mile the trail is layered with the rust-colored, long-needled clusters of the white pines. Across the pond you can see the beaver lodge, and here at marker 14-A is an abandoned lodge. Stay on the trail, since the extensive tunneling under the spongy shoreline can give way underfoot.

Marker 15 points out the bell-like yellow clintonia. A member of the lily family, this plant (like the Canada mayflower) has veined, shiny canoe-shaped leaves. Named for Governor DeWitt Clinton of New York, the flower has special symbolic importance—Clinton's father was instrumental in freeing Mother Ann, the founder of the Shakers during the colonial wars.

Two grown-in earth and stone bridges (markers 16 and 17) precede a stand of white ash. Ash trees are particularly strong and durable. This wood came in handy for fashioning tools, utensils, splits for bandboxes, and other Shaker projects. At 0.8 mile walkers come upon Factory Pond, north of Turning Mill Pond. This was one of the longest dams at Canterbury Shaker Village at the turn of the century, and a textile building was constructed here and outfitted with industrial looms.

It's interesting to note that while Vermont and New Hampshire farm women actually gained an education and independence from working at mills such as those at Lowell in Massachusetts, this type of automated work restricted Shaker women. Fancy work (weaving baskets, sewing, making boxes) had provided Shaker women an opportunity to move within the community. The variety of such daily duties as gathering herbs, baking bread, nursing the sick in the infirmary, weaving cloth, and selling Shaker products at fairs provided a much more rounded and healthy life than the assembly work at the Factory Mill, and eventually it was abandoned.

From Factory Pond turn right and walk the earthen dam rampart to an overgrown site where once there was an icehouse and woodworking mill. In fact, three mills were constructed in this area in addition to a twelve-foot-high wooden water wheel. It is long gone and the remains of the millrace are hidden by foliage. Earlier millraces were ditches lined with stone. But in 1905 this millrace (also known as the penstock) was a fifteen-inch iron pipe that conveyed water from the dam to a sluice-way, regulating the flow of the water. Trash racks were placed across the millrace to keep out debris and rocks that might seriously damage the water wheel.

Other terms for sluice are flume, fleam, or mill way. The sluice was the prewheel part of the operation. The postwheel water was directed into the mill pond via a milltail, tailrace, or spillway.

The water wheel at the Shaker dam was overshot, meaning that the water let in from the sluice gate hit the top of the wheel, which had more than two dozen paddles formed into buckets. The weight of the water falling from upper buckets into lower ones turned the wheel. Overshot wheels were 75 percent efficient, and wisely the Shakers installed the most effective wheel to operate the three mills here.

In effect, the Shakers worked twelve mills on a system of eight ponds. Factory, Turning, Saw, and Carding Mills all were connected on this side of the road. If "the old man's back went out," to put it in the language of the day, the lack of water power would have been disastrous to the community. Grain could not be ground. Cider could not be made. Lumber for building could not be sawed. Water for the brickyard would be in short supply. The community would have come to a standstill.

Marker 21 indicates Boys Island. This is really a peninsula jutting into Turning Mill Pond and once was planted with gardens but now is overgrown with black alder trees. Climb uphill on the trail from Factory Pond. Turn left onto the dirt road above the old granite pump house (marker 25). With the meadow wall now on your right, return to the herb gardens.

The buildings constructed, torn down, and rebuilt since the founding of this planned community in 1792 are well worth visiting. Whereas the tour represents the indoor spirit of the Shakers, the mill-pond trails demonstrate the outdoor life of the community. But no matter where you look, inside or out, the Shaker belief in "hands to work and hearts to God" is apparent.

The Creamery Restaurant sells Shaker-style meals; a gift shop offers Shaker furniture, boxes, and books. Tickets for the ninety-minute tour of the Shaker community may be purchased at the brick Admissions Building. You aren't required to take the tour if you walk a trail, but the tour is definitely worth fitting into your day at Canterbury.

Getting There

From I-93 take Exit 18 to NH 132 (with a sign to Shaker Village Historic Site). Turn left. Drive 0.6 mile. Take the right spur of a Y junction (with a sign to Canterbury). The roads are unmarked, but prominent signs to the town of Canterbury and Shaker Village point the way. Drive 0.5 mile to NH 132. After 0.1 mile on NH 132 (a continuation of the road you were on), at the next sign and median triangle turn left. Drive 1.0 mile, entering the town of Canterbury. At the public library is another Shaker Village sign. Continue past the library, driving another 3.8 miles. At the stop sign turn left. Drive 1.0 mile to the Shaker Village parking lot on the left. Total distance from I-93: about 7 miles.

Other Information

Canterbury Shaker Village (603-783-9511) is open daily 10:00 A.M. to 5:00 P.M. May through October and is open weekends November through April. Fee for ninety-minute tour inside the buildings. No fee for trail walks. Restaurant and gift shop available.

Canterbury Shaker Village
Meadow Pond Trail (Loop)
Canterbury

- **1.8 miles**
- **1 hour and 30 minutes**
- **moderate to difficult**

A wooded cart road leads to the shore of a wonderfully wild marsh and follows a brook and millrace, returning via cart road to Shaker Village.

A large, hidden marshy pond awaits you at the midpoint of this walk. The silence gives pause and walkers get a taste of wilderness rare in the modern world. To get there, walk behind the red brick Admissions Building parking lot. To the right of a large field is a dirt cart path. Descend gradually through the woods on this unblazed trail. A stone wall lines the trail on the right.

The tall gray trunks of white ash shoot straight upward. As a hardwood, ash is ideal for tools and implements. Shakers in the Church Family, which founded the community in 1792, hand-crafted ash into peg boards, chairs, and kitchen utensils. They wove thin splits of ash with palm leaf into hats and baskets.

After about a hundred yards on this wide forested path, you come to a clearing overgrown with a high

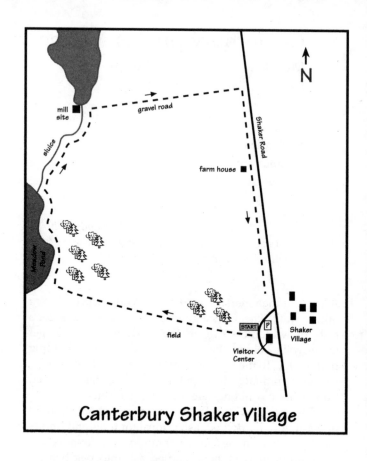

Canterbury Shaker Village

jungle of orange and gold jewelweed, a plant probably used in the Shaker infirmary to soothe the itch of insect bites and rashes from briars and poison ivy.

Beyond the field on the left, walk through a stand of hemlock. At 0.18 mile a faint trail comes in from the left.

Continue on the wide cart path, descending slightly to two granite posts standing as sentinels on each side of an entrance through a stone wall. These six-foot pillars designate most entries on Shaker property. These posts 0.2 mile deep in a forest probably joined two farm fields during the active years in the 1850s when 300 Shakers lived and worked the land.

The trail levels out at a planed log bridge through a muddy area. Several rusty gears, cans, saw blades, and machinery parts are scattered in dump sites along the way. Shakers lived simply—but the Industrial Revolution didn't pass them by. One day in 1810 Sister Tabitha Babbitt of the Harvard Shaker community sat at her spinning wheel and conceived of a circular saw blade run by water power that would be faster and more efficient than a vertical saw. She was right. Many other inventions and patents are attributed to Shakers. But increasingly as the community dwindled, members relied more heavily on manufactured goods from the outside world.

In the center of the trail we examined a *Ramaria,* or coral mushroom, past its prime and faded to a dull yellow, looking somewhat like a sponge. The name means "branched" and when we touched it, the vertical web of slender filaments broke away.

Slightly descending at 0.5 mile, you come in sight of the surprisingly expansive Meadow Pond. Walk between another set of monolithic granite pillars denoting an open entry in a stone wall. A split-log bench has been strategically placed beneath the boughs of a stately white pine so you can contemplate the beauty of this wilderness in quiet and serenity.

Granite posts mark wall openings and entrances at Canterbury Shaker Village.

At first we thought we must be seeing things when a pair of white swans floated from behind a blind of tall grass and reeds across the pond. Later, we discovered the staff had been looking for them and wished to return them closer to the village. Obviously, the swans were enjoying the summer—preening, nesting, and feeding on delectable roots and aquatic plants in utmost privacy. A great blue heron rose from the far shore, circled, and landed in a purple mat of pickerel weed.

Although it would be easy to sit here all day, continue the walk on a narrow path to the right, following the eastern shore. This is a grassy area filled in with swamp alder and swamp maples. At one time this was an open lake. As the edges grew in it evolved into a pond. Because of inlets clogged by waterlilies, cattails, and other water plants, the pond is evolving slowly into a marsh.

At 0.6 mile the footpath veers away from the pond and you pass through an opening in another stone wall. A hemlock trunk has been gnawed to an hourglass shape by beaver, and branches chewed by this large rodent are everywhere apparent in this northern reach of Meadow Pond.

Follow a wall on your right, descending to 0.75 mile. Cross through the same wall. On the left is another overlook from the north end of the pond. At 0.9 mile birders can take advantage of the grassy delta near Meadow

The circular saw was invented by a Shaker woman, and this rusting blade on Meadow Pond Trail tells of a bygone era at Canterbury Village.

Brook inlet to look for great blue heron, kingfisher, mallard, and other water birds.

Here you will see a handmade stone-lined sluice installed by the Shakers for runoff from a mill above this pond. In fall the sluice and banks of the brook are emblazoned with bright water-loving cardinal flowers.

The trail along this brook is overgrown, unblazed, and takes some patience as it disappears from view under the swaying tall grasses. The site of a stone foundation comes into view at 1.0 mile. From the riverbank one can see just what the Shaker pond system for water power involved.

Canterbury archives for 1824 record: "This year past we have been tareing down and bulding almost the whole time. We have built a dam to flow the Lake meddow and have made a brick yard in said meddow and halled building there for its convenience and dug clay and done a great deal more work on and about said meddow."

Ox and horse teams kept in the largest barn in New Hampshire (200 feet long) hauled stones for ditches, dams, and spillways such as those seen on this trail. Meadow Brook ditch joined an upper reservoir to the Meadow Lake below, providing water power for two sawmills from 1805 to 1850.

The trail winds uphill to the left beneath a great linden tree (identified by its large heart-shaped leaves) where it abuts a cart path. Walk a few yards to the left so you can observe the pond reservoir and a long beaver dam.

After surveying the layout of the mill, return to the right onto a coarse gravel cart road leading uphill.

At 1.17 miles, a faint dirt road comes in from the left. Ignore it and continue on the stone cartroad.

Ascend gradually between two meadows. To close the loop, at 1.5 miles turn right onto the main asphalt road that leads through upland farms and high mowings back to Canterbury Shaker Village. In another 0.3 mile you return to the parking lot.

Getting There

From I-93 take Exit 18 to NH 132 (with a sign to Shaker Village Historic Site). Turn left. Drive 0.6 mile. Take the right spur of a Y junction (with a sign to Canterbury). The roads are unmarked but prominent signs to the town of Canterbury and Shaker Village point the way. Drive 0.5 mile to NH 132. After 0.1 mile on NH 132 (a continuation of the road you were on), at the next sign and median triangle turn left. Drive 1.0 mile, entering the town of Canterbury. At the public library is another Shaker Village sign. Continue past the library, driving another 3.8 miles. At the stop sign turn left. Drive 1.0 mile to the Shaker Village parking lot on the left.

Other Information

Canterbury Shaker Village (603-783-9511) is open daily 10:00 A.M. to 5:00 P.M. May through October and is open weekends November through April. Fee for a ninety-minute tour of the village. No fee for trail walking.

Lang Pond Country Road & Libby Museum

Lang Pond Country Road Walk
Wolfeboro

- **3 miles (round-trip)**
- **2 hours (more including museum visit)**
- **moderate**

The historic road affords views of meadow, marsh, and Mirror Lake before ending at the Libby Museum on Lake Winnipesaukee.

This gravel-and-sand upcountry byway begins at the corner of NH 109A and Lang Pond Road and ends at Winter Harbor on Lake Winnipesaukee. Used frequently for recreation, the road in winter is popular with cross-country skiers and snowmobilers. In summer, it provides boat access to Mirror Lake and a pleasant walk in the country.

From the outset, both sides are lined with stone walls. A high mowing (upland pasture) spreads out to the left. Growing along the roadside are cinnamon ferns; they are named after the single fertile frond, emerging from the plant's base, which turns cinnamon brown in late spring. Hemlock, white pine, and sugar maple grow in the forest across from the pasture.

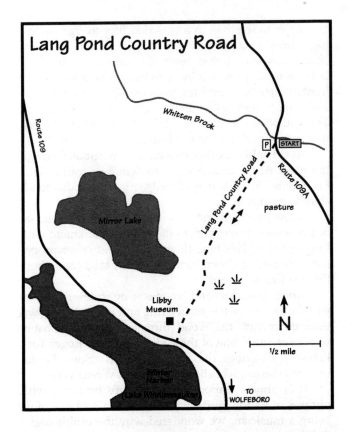

Lang Pond Country Road

At 0.2 mile, a culvert beneath the road accommodates one of several brook beds along the way.

An open corridor like this provides an excellent opportunity for identifying trees. At 0.3 mile on the right note the large, straight scaly trunks of hop hornbeam trees. They branch out in the opening above and are easier to see than in a crowded fifty-to-eighty-foot-high forest canopy. Another tree, the American hornbeam, has leaves that resemble those of a birch; it belongs to the same family. Also known as ironwood, its lumber once was used for tools requiring strength and endurance, such as mallets. Naturalist Henry David Thoreau observed that New England Indians fashioned their canoe paddles out of hornbeam.

At 0.5 mile, another culvert directs runoff beneath the road. At 0.6 mile a wide snowmobile trail crosses Lang Pond Road and is blazed with orange diamond-shaped markers.

A few paces beyond the crossroad, a dark green mat of periwinkle leaves covers the right embankment with long runners. This blue-flowered ground cover propagates by setting down runners, which take root where the tips touch the soil.

Wood thrushes and veeries sing from the deep woods. The veery has no eye ring and is a duller brown than its cousin, the wood thrush. But you probably won't see either one of these shy songsters. Roger Tory Peterson describes the veery voice as "Song liquid, breezy, ethereal, wheeling downward: vee-ur-vee-ur."

It is almost impossible to capture birdsong with phrases or words. Birdsong being music, and one of us being a musician, we wondered why the ornithologist didn't resort to musical notation. For instance, the veery sings a glissando (downward run) of eight to nine notes. The wood thrush, on the other hand, starts on a low note, sings a fifth or sixth higher (five to six notes), and then drops to a third. (Imagine a musical staff with an A, E, and middle C.) Peterson writes: "Listen for a flutelike ee-o-lay." The old sound logo for NBC comes closer to the tonal range than "ee-o-lay," but both fall miserably short of the range and tonal phrase of the wood thrush's majestic song.

A clearing at 0.7 mile shows a diversity of roadside plants. Sweet fern, a sun-loving plant that isn't a fern at all, takes over. It has long, narrow dark green blades with blunt projections, grows two to three feet tall and is a member of the bayberry family. It is characterized by a pungently sweet odor. Strawberries have put down their runners in this sandy location and one suspects another three-leaf plant isn't far away—poison ivy, which adores roadside sun and invariably grows in conjunction with berries in scrubby clearings such as this.

Within the vicinity of Mirror Lake, you might hear the distinctive sad complaint of a loon echoing over the water. We did. The loon has several calls. One is a somber unarticulated whistle of two notes about a fifth apart (C to G on the music staff). The second note is held (a long tone) and goes slightly flat (lowers a quarter tone) in the same way a train whistle trails off in the night. Although this call is heard most often around twilight, we heard it at midday.

A road to the east shore of Mirror Lake comes in at 1.1 miles, and the southern end of this clear fresh lake is visible in a few more feet. Water is channeled beneath the road to a marsh on the other side where spindly maples grow in the punky dark water. These are known as swamp maples, and their crimson leaves signal the beginning of fall foliage season in New Hampshire. Signage at a sandy beach and boat launch at 1.2 miles asks boaters to clean their crafts of milfoil, a freshwater

The Libby Museum on Lake Winnipesaukee provides a change of pace at the terminus of Lang Pond Country Road walk.

plant that clogs lakes, before entering Mirror Lake where it does not grow. Unfortunately, motorboats have access to this lovely lake where loons are nesting.

White pine lines the shore and the water is crystal clear. Surprisingly, in the nineteenth century the lake was dubbed "Dishwater Pond." At 1.3 miles walkers come to a double view and a wonderful example of how biodiversity and edge effects work. To your right is the lake, but take a look on the left at a sizable marsh. King-fisher dive for the minnows that spawn here and then migrate to lake water on the other side of the road. Nymph dragonflies and mosquitoes hatch from the marsh. Eventually they, too, fly to the lake, providing food for the larger fish. The shiny dark leaves of the purple-flowered pickerelweed provide still another refuge in spring for small fish, frogs, and turtles. Cattails pole-vault upward, their brown furry tops looking more like wieners on a stick than feline appendages. Along with rushes, reeds, and other grasses, they provide shelter for ducks and other water birds that feed on the open lake by day. And so these creatures commute from one habitat to another, in much the same way humans do.

To the right, Mirror Lake extends lengthwise toward the Ossipee Mountains in the north. Climb a gradual hill. Looking back and to the east you can make out the outline of Mount Whittier.

The road turns to blacktop at 1.5 miles, coming out at the Libby Museum fronting Winter Harbor on Lake Winnipesaukee.

A plaque explains that you have been walking on College Road. (See Chamberlain-Reynolds Memorial Forest, also on College Road, page 92.) In 1771 Governor John Wentworth and the King's Council voted a highway be built from Wolfeboro to Hanover. In August of the same year the governor rode sixty-seven miles through Plymouth and Groton, past Goose Ponds and over Moose Mountain, to the first commencement at Dartmouth College.

Take time to stop at the Libby Museum, designed and opened by Henry Forrest Libby in 1912. Libby had a voracious curiosity about everything from dentistry, chemistry, and taxonomy to natural history, botany, and geology. Everyone will find something of interest in the diverse collections of this one-room exhibition hall.

Getting There

In Wolfeboro at the junction of NH 28 north/109 south, drive 0.5 mile on NH 28 north/109 south and turn north (left) onto NH 109A at Wolfeboro Falls. Drive 4 miles, turn left onto Lang Pond Road, and park to the side near a stone wall.

Other Information

Libby Museum (603-569-1035) is open 10:00 A.M. to 4:00 P.M. Closed Mondays. Nominal fee.

Knights Pond
Conservation Area
Knights Pond & Peninsula (Loop)
South Wolfeboro

- **2.4 miles**
- **1 hour and 15 minutes**
- **moderate**

Two worlds in one walk: first, a wild, isolated pond shoreline, then a peninsula overview of an extensive beaver marsh.

A keen sense of being separate from the busy, noisy world adds to the adventure of this site. Pass behind the gate and walk downhill through beech and oak forest on the sandy access road to the pond beach at 0.4 mile. (On the way you will pass by one of the trailheads to the 1.7-mile Main Trail around the marsh and pond.) Knights Pond nestles in white pines, its dark secluded surface mirroring the sky and trees. The first glimpse can be breathtaking.

At the beach turn right and follow light blue blazes to the right onto the other trailhead of the Main Trail Loop.

Blueberries crop close to the pond water, colored nearly black by tannin from submerged logs and pine needles. After a short, steep uphill climb at 0.5 mile, you

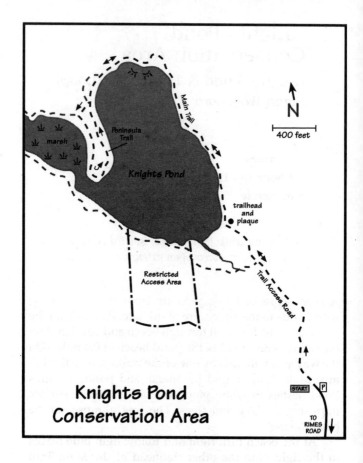

**Knights Pond
Conservation Area**

Labels in map: N, 400 feet, Main Trail, Peninsula Trail, marsh, Knights Pond, trailhead and plaque, Restricted Access Area, Trail Access Road, START, P, TO RIMES ROAD

come to a hemlock glade. All along the pond are members of the heath family. These bushes like water and grow in boggy sections. Sheep laurel, with blue-green oblong leaves, has an interesting background. Sheep that survive browsing on its toxic foliage become addicted and lead farmers to the plants, which can then be eradicated. Leatherleaf is another tough laurel of the New Hampshire pond and bog terrain. It, too, has the gray green oblong leaves characteristic of this family.

If you startled a great blue heron at the inlet at 0.8 mile, keep still and this prehistoric-looking, slate gray bird may circle around on broad, slow-flapping wings to land again. In New Hampshire it seems as if every pond, river, and stream supports at least one of these majestic crested herons, which feast on fish, frogs, and salamanders. They stand tall on spindly legs, prowling slowly, freezing as they spy prey, then zap! Nabbing a dinner with long, spearlike bills.

At a grassy clearing labeled Picnic Area on the Conservation Trust map, a tote road enters from the right. We suggest that you save picnics or snacks for the boulders on Peninsula Loop. In season the grass harbors disease-bearing ticks.

Walk on stones through a muddy pass grown in with cinnamon and sensitive fern (the latter fern, with broad, scalloped yellowish fronds, is named "sensitive" because the first frost kills it). At 0.92 mile cross a log footbridge over another inlet.

At 1.0 mile look for a double blaze indicating a detour that goes left uphill and down. Don't take it. Continue to parallel the pond shore.

At the next double blaze, however, veer right and away from the lake. In about thirty yards (within sight of a marsh) turn left. You can barely make out a white blaze on an oak tree to the left—directly opposite huge boulders on the right.

Now you're on the short Peninsula Loop above the marsh, and at 1.1 miles you approach a beaver house. Beyond, a serpentine river of open water channels through the reeds and grasses. Loaf-shaped boulders top the peninsula hill. At 1.2 miles you can sit on one of them at the tip and observe the pond on the left and the marsh on the right, with a channel in between.

A marsh wren wags its tail and feeds on a huckleberry. Or a heron wades in slow motion through the pickerel weed. At twilight, you may spot a beaver swimming stealthily through the dark water, its fur sleeked back and beady eyes on the alert.

Dominating the horizon behind the pond beach rise the dramatic cliff faces of Mount Longstack.

To close the Peninsula Loop, keep the pond to your right, following white blazes past a tall white birch and a boulder with a distinctive crack in it at 1.4 miles. Expanding ice often fractures these geological monoliths along prominent faults in the granite.

Here the trail narrows to the size of a balance beam, so watch your step. Pine needles can be slippery and the descent from the hill on the peninsula is steep.

Continue along the shore with the water a few feet to the right. At 1.5 miles recross the log footbridge. Retrace the blue-blazed Main Trail back to the beach access road (always keeping the pond to your right).

It's uphill all the way back on the access road, but at least you aren't dragging a boat. (Fishermen and canoe owners are asked to portage nonmotorized boats the 0.8 mile.)

The Conservation Trust flier relates "A Remarkable Protection Story" involving the Wolfeboro Chapter of

Knight's Pond is an isolated gem in a wilderness setting.

the Conservation Trust, Land Conservation Investment Program, Trust for New Hampshire Lands, Fish and Game Department, and private landowners and volunteers. Five parcels of land around the pond were secured and purchased.

A set of guidelines reminds the public that protection continues with them. Carry out what you carry in. Park in designated areas.

"Dogs must be kept under control"; we would amend this to read "Dogs should be kept at home." Walkers prefer finding deer scat on a trail, not dog-do, and even leashed dogs scare away most wildlife.

"Motorized off-road vehicles are prohibited." Unfortunately, snowmobiling is permitted on the access road, the pond, and at the north end of the pond. To our way of thinking, snowmobiles are equally damaging to a pond environment. They pollute the air with noise and noxious gas fumes, as well as scare away the wildlife.

Summer walking on Knights Pond is as good as it gets. But in the fall during duck and deer seasons, we suggest you walk on other property "protected" from hunters.

Getting There

From the blinker at South Wolfeboro on NH 28, drive south 1.6 miles to Stagecoach Road. Turn left and drive 1.1 miles. At a Y junction bear left on Rines Road. Drive 0.5 mile to the Knights Pond Conservation Area sign and a gate on the left. Pass through this gate (closed December through April) and drive another 0.5 mile to the parking lot and another gate. The access (also closed December through April) road to the pond begins here.

Affiliated Organizations

Lakes Region Conservation Trust (Wolfeboro Chapter)
P.O. Box 2235
Wolfeboro, NH 03894

Ryefield Marsh

Ellie's Woodland Walk

South Wolfeboro

- **0.5 mile**
- **30 minutes**
- **easy**

A short and sweet boardwalk stroll alongside an
extensive marsh full of aquatic plants and bird life
to a platform overlooking the scene.

The charm of this short walk across from Lake Wentworth State Beach is the discovery of the multifaceted
aquatic life that resides and grows here. Once sufficient-
ly away from Route 109, sections of the lakeside marsh
appear through a thin line of bordering trees at the
beginning and then through tall grasses and shrubs farther along.

First, pick up a descriptive flier in the roadside mailbox where a stone marker signals the trailhead. A plaque
reads: Ellie's Woodland Walk. This land was given to the
town of Wolfeboro by Eloise Linscott 1897–1978 in the
interest of conservation forever.

Follow the Walk arrow on a white-pine tree trunk
growing at the roadside trailhead on the right. This
points toward the dirt road off the highway and in 100

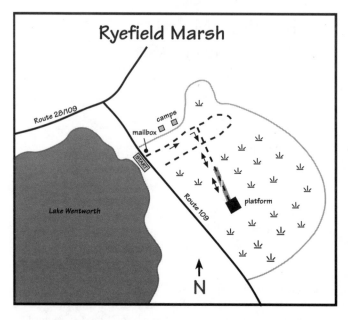

Ryefield Marsh

feet takes you among three small cabins before moving into the woods. (You aren't trespassing; you have a right of way to Ellie's Walk.)

In 500 feet turn right on a worn grassy road. No blazes are needed here; the roadway is obvious.

At 0.15 mile cross a road and proceed straight ahead on a corridor of mixed young pasture pine and small gray birch, the so-called "poverty" birch that grow in sandy soil.

A little later walk across a wooden footbridge with a right-hand railing over a sluiceway filled on the right with pickerelweed, waterlilies, grasses, and alders. On the left side of the bridge lies a long, wonderful view of the marsh with water flowing under the bridge toward Lake Wentworth.

At 0.2 mile a short distance farther, a slightly spongy but safe boardwalk stretches flat across a short section of open marsh (be careful stepping along the board; some of the planks are weak and, when we were there, needed repair).

This boardwalk section places you in the heart of the marsh, up close with many water-loving plants. At the end of the boardwalk a slightly raised platform perches you high enough to peer over the tips of the tall grasses for a wide-angle view of the intriguing scene.

Most influential in creating the marsh are the industrious beaver and the dam they constructed to protect their wattle and daub lodges. Drainpipes have been installed (by humans) so that a constant water level is maintained in order to protect nests that otherwise would be submerged and food supplies eliminated for many species.

This Wolfeboro Conservation Area has an impressive list of wildlife seen in and around Ryefield Marsh. The fascinating habitat supports water bugs, salamanders, fish, aquatic plants, beaver, muskrat, deer, skunk, raccoon, turtles, northern water snakes, moose, squirrel, owls, wood ducks, ruffed grouse, woodpeckers, chickadees, great blue herons, red-winged blackbirds, and many other winged and web-footed creatures.

Plant life growing in and around the marsh includes sweet fern, raspberries, arrowhead, pickerelweed, sedge grass, marsh fern, and marsh loosestrife.

You might see a dark-brown muskrat. This aquatic rodent measures up to fourteen inches long and weighs two to three pounds. It swims with its long slender tail trailing behind and showing on the water surface, distinguishing it from beaver, which swim with their noses and eyes scarcely visible. The larger aquatic beaver measure up to four feet long, weigh approximately sixty pounds, and are known for the loud "slap" of their broad, flat tails on the water surface as a warning to their neighbors.

Probably the best time to see wildlife in this and other large marshes is in the quiet of very early morning or late evening when other humans are less likely to rustle up noise in the area. But you never know, especially in active marshes like that of Ryefield. High noon may stir up turtles to the shore or logs, yellow-bellied

Ducks find the tubers of these white-flowered arrowheads a tasty treat.

sapsuckers pecking at sapwells for the sweets of birch trees, scurrying squirrels in nearby oak trees, trout jumping for buzzing mosquitoes. If any complex natural habitat requires a persistent, watchful eye, a marsh ranks high.

Return to your car by the same route.

Getting There

From NH 28 north/109 in Wolfeboro drive 3.2 miles. Turn right at the sign to Wentworth Beach. Drive 1.7 miles. The sign for Ellie's Woodland Walk is on the left. Park on the lake side of the road.

Affiliated Organization

The Wolfeboro Conservation Commission
P.O. Box 629
Wolfeboro, NH 03894

Abenaki Tower

Abenaki Tower Walk
Wolfeboro/Melvin Village

- **0.3 mile**
- **20 minutes**
- **easy**

---

*A bird's-eye view from a 100-foot tower of the inlets
and coves of Lake Winnipesaukee and the
Ossipee Mountains to the north.*

The early Abenaki, also known as the Dawn People,
lived in summer encampments along the shore of Lake
Winnipesaukee and other lakes of this region. Abenaki
Tower overlooks the wide blue lake and, in name at
least, honors these native residents and their presence on
the lake, which they called "beautiful water in a high
place."

Behind the parking area, a dirt tote road winds
uphill through mixed oak, maple, and pine forest. The
climb is gradual, easy, and shaded.

Coarse common bracken ferns, with horizontal lay-
ers of (often) four-foot-long tripart fronds, line the roadside, preferring sun to shade. Bison-sized boulders
emerge from the dark woodland, their girth even more
impressive when one realizes they were deposited by a

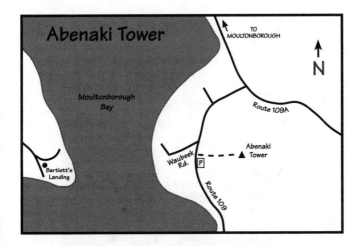

Abenaki Tower

Moultonborough
Bay

TO
MOULTONBOROUGH

N

Route 109A

Abenaki
Tower

Waubeek
Rd.

P

Route 109

Bartlett's
Landing

slowly grinding ice sheet carrying them from the mountains to the north.

In 0.1 mile you've arrived at the tower built from huge criss-crossed pine trunks. Tall northern red (Norway) pine are ideal for constructions such as this. The 100-foot-high observation tower was dedicated in 1978 and is "maintained voluntarily by local residents (The Abenaki Tower Association, Melvin Village), who desire to share its view and beauty with friends and visitors."

Getting to the top involves forty-eight steps covering three stories—the last being extremely steep. We suggest those suffering from acrophobia turn back, and children should be accompanied by sure-footed adults.

But, oh, what views! Directly across Moultonborough Bay are Bartlett's and Jonathan's Landings on Long Island. Beyond, way across the lake, are "The Weirs," where Native Americans used to spread seines to catch

Abenaki Tower overlooks Lake Winnipesaukee.

spawning salmon in early spring. Evidence has been found of groups of Paleo-Indian hunters on the lake as early as 11,200 years ago. Apparently, the points and blades discovered at this site were used by migratory hunters to kill caribou (and possibly mastodon or mammoth). Native Americans camped at this same spot at least 3,000 years ago, fishing the inlets with a system of woven hemp-and-brush fish traps called "weirs" in W and V shapes across the narrow outlet between Lake

Winnipesaukee and Lake Paugus. Impressive artifacts from more recent tribes (ca. 1600) with summer encampments on the shores of central New Hampshire lakes may be seen at the Libby Museum of Natural History (see p. 66), the Indian Museum at Kearsarge (see p. 162), and at the New Hampshire History Museum (Eagle Court in Concord).

The glistening white facades of Melvin Village peek through the densely wooded shoreline to the immediate north and then beyond to the Ossipee and Sandwich Mountain ranges. Eastern and southern views are grown in, at least during the summer months.

From above, the sumac groves around the tower clearing, bushy crowns of oak, and deep greenery of hemlock fill in the foreground.

As they say, what goes up must come down. We've discovered the dismount from the tower is facilitated by backing down step by step while holding onto both of the stair rails.

Return via the tote road (which is closed to vehicles). This walk is short and sweet, with grand views from the room at the top.

Getting There

From Melvin Village: Drive approximately 2 miles south on NH 109 past a country club on the right. A mortared stone sign reading Abenaki Tower is prominent on the left.

From Wolfeboro: From the bridge at the center of town, drive 8 miles north on NH 109. A stone mortared signpost designates a parking area on the right.

Russel C. Chase Bridge Falls

Bridge Falls Urban Trail
Wolfeboro

- **0.75 mile**
- **30 minutes**
- **easy**

An "urban" trail extending from the downtown center of activity and along the abandoned Wolfeboro railroad bed and Back Bay shoreline to an old mill.

A prime example of an abandoned railroad bed transformed into an enjoyable walkway, this footpath takes people in short order from the center of town into a natural setting of water and woods. Be aware that occasionally bicyclists cruise this trail as well as local residents on regular "power" walks for fitness. The openness of the pathway lets you see and hear a lot on the brief excursion.

A sign at the trailhead behind the old railroad depot marks the entrance. The path is a cooperative project of the National Park Service of the U.S. Department of the Interior and the New Hampshire Department of Resources and Economic Development. At the start of the trail on the left is an aging red building identified as the "Wolfeboro Oil Co., Inc., Warehouse—1872."

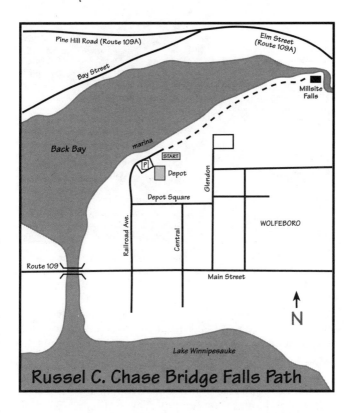

Russel C. Chase Bridge Falls Path

The path is so well designed in its simplicity and aesthetics that the urge to keep on going prevails. Right away you'll enter a well-spaced corridor of young ornamental trees planted alongside the pathway—the lacy tree of heaven, silvery Russian olives, and others. A few more strides and on the right a moist pocket of land supports pink-blossomed loosestrife growing straight,

A few yards from Wolfeboro's Main Street traffic, walkers, joggers, and bikers can enjoy a back bay of Winnipesaukee.

tall, and narrow. Pretty as it is, the loosestrife is an unwelcome interloper, a European invader notorious for overwhelming and dominating native plants. In the fall, loosestrife is joined by the yellow-headed goldenrod, which also favors open wet areas and roadsides.

At this point cross the little-used asphalt road and continue straight ahead on the trail. This section is a kind of buffer zone between the many town buildings behind you and the more natural setting at the end of the walk. On the right appears a grassy playing field and baseball diamond, on the left a small marina for modest-sized boats.

This section provides benches to sit and enjoy the casual boating activity coming and going on Back Bay, as it's called locally. (In reality, this is the mouth of the

Smith River.) Overhead lights have been installed near the benches and along the path for summer-night strolls by the shoreline. Listen day and evening for steamer whistles that sound now and then in the distance on Lake Winnipesaukee.

At 0.23 mile the trail continues on an old railroad bed past boulders on the left at first, then the right. This part of the path takes you near more trees, especially some tall white pine. The mixture of boulder and pine has been designed to enhance shade and variety. A little farther a staghorn sumac grove sends up its tan, fuzzy, antler-like branches. The sumac is easy to identify from its dozen long and narrow leaves and upright, cone-clustered maroon berries. Sumac leaves equal red swamp maples for their brilliance during fall foliage season.

At 0.39 mile the remains of the Berry Excelsior Mill in Wolfeboro Falls appear. Walk through a gate onto a wooden platform with a bench and table. Water flows beneath it from the right. The abandoned antique wooden building has weathered gray. This makes a pleasant site for an al fresco lunch or snack near the falls cascading into Smith River.

The end of this pathway is NH 28. A sign across the road reading Recreation Trail identifies a continuation of this abandoned railroad bed to Wakefield used by snowmobilers, mountain bikers, and hikers.

Getting There

The trailhead is located directly behind the renovated railroad depot one block east of Main Street in the center of Wolfeboro. Park in the adjoining lot.

Squam Lake Beach/ Chamberlain-Reynolds Memorial Forest

Squam Lake Beach Trail

Center Harbor

- **1.2 miles**
- **1 hour**
- **moderate**

*A forest-to-beach walk on a tote road and
narrow footpath passing through rich woodlands
to a secluded tree-lined cove "On Golden Pond."*

Squam Lake was always special before this sumptuous
cove-filled body of deep blue water became nationally
known as the site of the 1981 movie *On Golden Pond*.
Although some motels and tourist attractions have capi-
talized on the movie fame, this walk offers something
better—a diverse woodland stroll to one of Squam's isolated green-and-blue pockets of repose.

The forest preserve is owned by the New England
Forestry Foundation and named in honor of two natu-
ralists dedicated to sustaining the best of New
Hampshire—Allen Chamberlain (1867–1945) and Harris
A. Reynolds (1883–1953).

The trailhead begins to the immediate left of the large
signboard. In the woods, a visitor sign-in book inside a

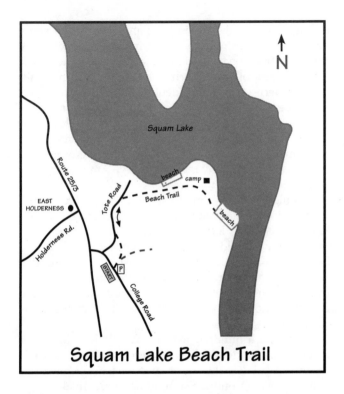

Squam Lake Beach Trail

pedestal box marks a junction to Beaches Campsites to the right down a tote road and Ant Hill Trail to the left. Take the trail to the left and walk along a needle-strewn path through a spacious tree farm of red pine. Walking on a slight downslope makes an enjoyable beginning. In 0.16 mile you cross a two-step-wide brook (cross on solid, dry stones) and at 0.19 mile pass a giant white pine on the left.

At 0.21 mile turn right onto a tote road and follow the occasional yellow blazes on the right downward through some high-growing cinnamon ferns; the name derives from the single spore-bearing frond, which turns dry and cinnamon colored in the spring. Along here look for examples of sweet fern, which isn't a fern at all. Called a fern for popular identification, this plant with frondlike branches and rows of deep green, oblong, fern-like leaves is not a spore-bearing fern but a flowering member of the bayberry family. Sweet fern roots use actinomycetes bacteria to fix nitrogen from ground soil; its leaves were used by regional Native Americans as an additive to smoking tobacco.

Along the road-trail, mostly under spacious white pine, notice the many tall, orange-and-yellow jewelweed blossoms as well as the low-lying red berries of the bunchberry ground cover. Midheight red beads of the hobblebush in late summer are conspicuous along this section, too; they turn deep purple later on. A viburnum, the hobblebush begins its season in April with lacy white clusters of flowers that seem to float above their saucer-sized leaves.

In about a hundred feet the Middle Meadow Trail enters from the right. Here, too, a marker post indicates Swamp Walk to the right and Beaches Campsites straight ahead. Continue straight down the road.

At 0.26 mile the road-trail moves into a more open area (some trees have been thinned here), with many white pine towering above. A short distance ahead on the right at 0.29 mile, a vertical marker reads Beaches Campsites in white letters. Take this footpath that heads into more dense woodlands with increased brush at leg level for a short distance. A yellow blaze appears soon on the right. Here look for patches of mountain laurel low to the ground. This evergreen shrub flourishes in

A pristine cove "On Golden Pond."

acid soil and is a welcome, omnipresent plant in New Hampshire, where its many cuplike pink and white clusters flower at lower elevations in May, making this member of the heath family a vanguard of spring after the long winter months. Also called calico bush, sturdy mountain laurel branches and leaves were once used by chimney sweeps for their brooms to brush soot buildup from wood-stove chimneys.

At 0.41 mile and a Y junction, proceed left. Squam Lake now comes into view between shoreline trees. The woods open up and the mountain laurel is plentiful.

In short order, veer left at another Y junction at 0.45 mile, and soon you're at a narrow sandy beach. Rocky-edged islands covered with thick woods, houseless convoluted inlets of undisturbed waters, and deep blue surfaces everywhere in front of you make this a rewarding destination.

Return the few yards on the shore access trail and proceed beside the lake until you see to the left, at 0.54 mile, a point of land with a lean-to shelter of logs under a canopy of a few pines. A canoe dock lies a little farther to the right. Respect the privacy of campers blessed with this idyllic spot.

Continue along the shoreline past this small camp clearing and walk down a story of flat-stone steps beside large boulders on the right to a larger beach cove at 0.6 mile. A shallow roped-off swimming area is located here. At this point we heard a loon. Maybe you'll see one.

To return, go back along the shoreline with the Squam on the right, pass the lean-to, and get on the same main trail. Follow the marker posts reading Parking West.

Getting There

From 0.2 mile south of East Holderness Road on US 3 heading south turn left onto College Road. Drive 0.4 mile and park in a small clearing under a large maple tree and in front of a prominent signboard.

From Center Harbor drive 3.1 miles on NH 25B north. Turn right and drive north on US 3 and NH 25 for 0.8 mile. Turn right on College Road and drive 0.4 mile to the large signboard and maple tree at the small parking area on the left. For more information, call 603-253-4582.

Sidney Smith Woodland (SPNHF)

Sidney Smith Woodland Trail (Loop)
Tuftonboro

- **0.9 mile**
- **45 minutes**
- **moderate**

A relatively undeveloped cove of the lake lends a deep, quiet character to this forested Tuftonboro Neck property.

Although you start this trail near a few lakeside cottages and in a residential area, a feeling of isolation soon envelops you. Pass behind the gate and follow the Trail sign and yellow metal blazes. Veer to the right, passing a rock pile on the left and winding downhill through a considerable stand of tall red oak. You can identify red oak from the jagged edges of the leaves, but gazing overhead, it's difficult to make out the exact contour of the leaves against the sky. Leaf mulch might provide a clue. However, the quickest way to distinguish red oak from other oaks is to examine the bark of the trunk. The inner grooves have a red tinge, while the outer bark is gray.

Cross a mud/stone slough and climb a hill grown in with wood ferns, birches, and the ubiquitous carpet of club moss found in moist woodland. These 1-to-2-inch

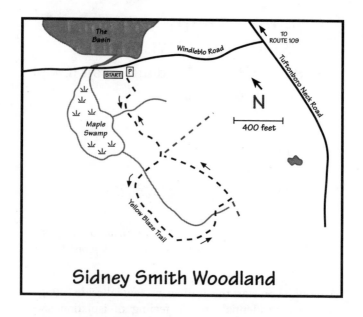

Sidney Smith Woodland

evergreen club-shaped plants don't look very imposing today, but they are related to club mosses that grew 100 feet tall 50 million years ago!

At 0.2 mile turn right and pass through an opening in a stone wall. This property, like much of New Hampshire land, once was cleared for farming. But as industrial development moved jobs from the farm to the factory, the farmland was abandoned. After 1900 the farms slowly were replaced by summer estates along the shores of Lake Winnipesaukee. Pioneer geologist Philip Smith and his wife, Lenore, an educator and librarian in Washington, D.C., moved to a summer place here. The sixty-acre woodland was donated to the Society for the

Protection of New Hampshire Forests by their son Sidney in the 1980s.

Turn left, following the Loop Trail sign a few yards beyond a venerable old paper birch. These birch are commonly referred to as canoe birch because the waterproof bark was used by Native Americans in the north for their canoes. These canoes still are crafted in the northern woods, though fiberglass and noisy aluminum by and large have replaced them.

White birch is short lived and shallow rooted.

From 0.4 mile to 0.5 mile is another muddy fen with ferns that turn the walk into rock hopscotch for a few yards. Bright green, shiny Christmas ferns (about two feet high) protrude in clusters from rock crevices. The Christmas fern is so named because it grows evergreen under the snow through the holidays; also, the base of the blades have Christmas stocking shapes. Common cinnamon ferns rise above the Christmas ferns; they grow in symmetrical whorls up to five feet high.

This ferny fen is connected to a maple swamp to the right of the trail—barely visible through the trees. Pass by the trunk of a friendly old sugar maple on the left side of the trail. When this area was farmland stone walls bordered the pastures; often, a tree like this was left in the pasture as shade for sheep and cattle.

For a while enjoy the hemlock needles on the trail. Now parallel a stone wall to the right. Loop around and pass through an opening in the wall at 0.6 mile.

At 0.63 mile you will pass through an opening in another stone wall. To the left of the trail is a logged area with a few lone white pine still standing in the airy clearing.

Swing downhill and at 0.7 mile follow a sign reading To Windleblo Road. By 0.8 mile you have returned to the rock/mud slough traversed at the beginning. Climb uphill at the double blaze. Now the red maple swamp is on the left. Red, or swamp, maples take root in water and don't look like much except in fall. They are the first to turn colors when cold nights set in, and they glow a spectacularly bright crimson. This is an ideal place to catch them in all their glory—with the blue water of Lake Winnipesaukee in the distance.

At a second double blaze, bear left; suddenly the magnificent quiet lake basin comes into view. After the leaves have fallen, the view expands even farther across Winter Harbor and to the east.

Getting There

From Wolfeboro drive on NH 109 north 4.4 miles. Turn left on Tuftonboro Neck Road, driving 0.6 mile. Turn right on Windleblo Road and drive 0.2 mile to the Society for the Protection of New Hampshire Forests sign on the left. A few yards farther on the left is a gate and narrow pull-off opposite a basin of Lake Winnipesaukee.

Affiliated Organizations

Society for the Protection of New Hampshire Forests
54 Portsmouth Street
Concord, NH 03301
603-224-9945

Gertrude K. & Edward E. Hoyt Jr. Audubon Preserve

Esker & Beaver Trail (Loops)

East Madison

- **1.75 miles**
- **1 hour**
- **moderate**

A well-conceived series of trails on an esker ridge overlooking a glacial kettle pond, past a beaver lodge, and skirting an extensive heath.

From the outset this trail promises a fascinating walk, and by the time you finish the enjoyable figure-eight loop the promises come true. Eskers, kettle-hole ponds, beaver lodges, intriguing woods, and more—the diversity here in a relatively small space is very rewarding.

Begin at the gate with a mailbox of guide maps available on the left. Start out on the yellow-blazed path as it curves right upward slightly past an old cabin on the right and the lower end of Purity Lake on the left. Continue to the polished, trailside granite bench on the right—inscribed 1907, Ellen Hoyt Gillard, 1989.

The trail narrows to a footpath across the top of a meandering esker. These snakelike ridges of grown-over sand and gravel make wonderful trails through

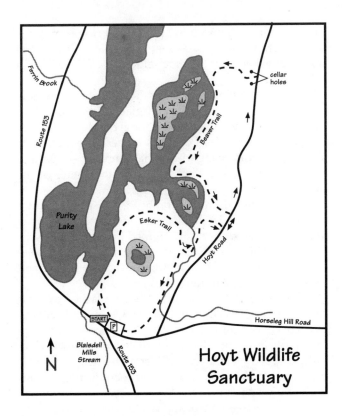

Hoyt Wildlife Sanctuary

woodlands; you can see both sides of the terrain below as you stroll along. In fact, from this esker you get a bird's-eye view at the wooden post marker 2 of No Bottom Pond to the right.

Eskers were formed during the last ice age. As mature glaciers melted, streams of water formed inside them. These huge streams carried debris that piled on the "stream bed" into these pyramidal ridges measuring sometimes up to 100 feet high. New England is noted for eskers, but they are seldom seen elsewhere in this country.

No Bottom Pond is a kettle-hole pond. Kettle-hole ponds resulted when blocks of glacial ice settled into sediment. The ice melted, forming ponds up to fifty feet deep. No Bottom Pond has turned into a bog, the signature plant being the sphagnum moss matting growing thicker and thicker toward the center of the pond.

At 0.2 mile from the trailhead, the path narrows again and descends slightly into an unexpected open area that looks haphazardly clipped by cosmic-size scissors. In reality a small, powerful tornado smashed through here in 1980, snapping great trees in half and ransacking the rest of this small section.

The process of regenerating the whiplashed parcel is called succession. With sunlight now admitted without tree cover, certain "pioneers" grow here—sweet fern (not a true fern, but this wax myrtle looks somewhat like one), raspberry vines and wild strawberries, scrub oak, bracken fern. As the regeneration proceeds, these plants will give way to new members of the family trees that were destroyed—red oak and white pine.

Continue along the top of the esker and soon you're back under tree cover. On the left appears a wonderful backwater marsh formed by a beaver dam. The scene stops you in your tracks—cattails, tall grasses, a twisting stream shifting through plant life in the marsh surrounded by snags (standing dead trees). In a beaver marsh, snags usually are pines, which beaver favor least and eat last. Beaver prefer poplar, aspen, alder, willow, birch, and maple before pines.

Proceeding down the esker, take the red-blazed trail on the left at 0.4 mile. In less than another tenth of a mile downward, follow the single switchback on the trail to cross Little Brook. In 200 feet pass by an old dump and continue 300 feet more to emerge onto Hoyt Road, a hard-packed dirt byway through the woods.

At this point, turn left and bypass in 100 feet the re-entry trail to the woods. Instead, continue along the road with yellow blazes on tree trunks on the left side of the road.

In a quarter-mile, look on the left for the remains of a field-stone cellar hole. In about five yards more, turn left to re-enter the trail into the woods. The name has been changed from Heath View Trail to Beaver Trail (you'll notice the sign). Follow the wide old tote road downhill and in 0.2 mile veer to the left where a yellow blaze is nailed to a birch tree and the trail narrows to a footpath.

Alongside the path you pass a lot of maple-leaf viburnum as well as low-lying bunchberry and winter-green. An isolated one-time section of Purity Lake comes into sight on the right and is known as The Heath. This is a floating island of sphagnum moss and other vegetation. Good frog country, which means good chances of spotting a long-legged great blue heron standing motionless waiting for supper. Frozen, this tall wader stalks its dinner, then suddenly the long S-shaped neck unwinds and the beak at the end closes on the unsuspecting prey.

A newly constructed beaver lodge in the Hoyt Audubon Preserve.

The trail curves to the left and ascends slightly, passing a sign on a large tree reading Red Oak, the predominant oak in the White Mountains and much of the rest of the state.

For the next 500 feet the trail skirts the edge of the beaver marsh that you saw from the esker earlier in the walk. Up close here, you can see branchy details of the stick-and-mud beaver lodge. Maybe a furry scout will be swimming to and fro to see what you're up to.

What you can't see is the cache of branches and twigs stored underwater for winter food.

Notice as you curve left away from the beaver lodge a wooden birdhouse on a post with a metal umbrella near the top to protect inhabitants from marauding squirrels and other pirates.

As you walk along the left bank of the marsh and uphill toward the woods, be sure to stop and do an about-face. This panorama of marsh and beaver lodge is one of the most memorable wild scenes preserved so carefully here.

Proceed on the trail and emerge onto Hoyt Road again. The Beaver Trail loop (the top half of the entire figure-eight trail) covers 0.9 mile.

Turn right and continue down the road 100 feet. At the red arrow blaze, turn right from the road and enter the woods again. Proceed down the red-blazed trail. (The remaining trail to the parking area covers 0.3 mile.)

In 200 feet, past the old dump you saw earlier, cross Little Brook again. Return up the single switchback to the top of the esker, following the red blazes to the junction with the yellow-blazed trail.

At this junction (0.2 mile from the road) turn left and follow the yellow blazes.

This esker is the continuation of the same one you walked at the outset of the trail. It curves through the woods and measures fifteen feet across along here.

You're walking an esker in much the same way Native Americans did, using high ground to keep out of marsh on either side. Eskers are used another way today—mined for the clean gravel inside them, which in the process, of course, destroys the formations.

Follow the yellow blazes as the trail veers left and then quickly right before descending a steep, short bank to the parking field and trailhead.

Getting There

From the junction of NH 25 and NH 153 in Effingham Falls, drive north on NH 153 for 5.3 miles. Turn right at Horseleg Hill Road. If you pass Purity Lake Resort in East Madison (on the left of NH 153), you've missed the turn off (about 0.2 mile from the resort). Hoyt Sanctuary is on the left of Horseleg Hill Road immediately after you've made the turn. Park on the two-rut road in the roadside field near the trail sign.

Affiliated Organizations

Audubon Society of New Hampshire
3 Silk Road
Concord, NH 03301
603-224-9909

Castle Springs

Falls of Song Footpath

Moultonborough

- **0.25 mile**
- **20 minutes**
- **easy**

---

*A wide, manicured path to an up-close observation platform
at the river pool of an impressive fifty-foot waterfall.*

Requiring little effort, this entrancing walk is like a fantasy scene from a fairy tale. Park to the right of the access road to Castle in the Clouds on the 2,215-foot summit of Bald Peak. Halfway up the entrance road a ten-foot-wide footpath leads to an impressive fifty-foot ribbon waterfall.

To the right is a snag or dead standing tree trunk, riddled with holes made by woodpeckers, flycatchers, and other long-billed birds looking for insects in the punky wood. Snags aren't important only to birds: wild bees often use them as hives. Unfortunately, landowners and loggers in New England are destroying these invaluable natural homes for bees, birds, and small mammals.

To the left of the footpath are tall, majestic hemlocks. Notice how the base of the tree embraces the rock lodged in the steep cliff bank. Though tree trunks can't move,

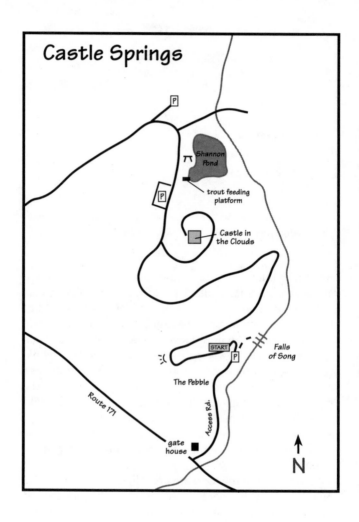

Castle Springs

P

Shannon
Pond

trout feeding
platform

P

Castle in
the Clouds

START   P   Falls
of Song

The Pebble

Route 171

Access Rd.

gate
house

N

hemlocks often engulf any object in their way—including rocks and boulders, which offer a foundation for their shallow roots.

Over the railing on the right you can peer into the deep channel carved by the relentless dynamo of the river. On the far riverside, children will probably spy dark caves. The Ossipee Indians, a tribe of the Penacook Confederacy, frequented this area. It is possible these caves have been a refuge for mammals such as black bear as well as man.

In 1913 Thomas Plant sold his $21 million shoe business and bought up all the land from this part of the Ossipee Mountains to Lake Ossipee. Part of his acquisition included a 5,000-acre private park, originally owned by B. F. Shaw. Shaw, who had built a one-mile road to the top of the mountain, charged the public twenty-five cents for use of the park.

Plant had a different vision for the land. He created a private golf course and country club, and hired 1,000 Italian stone masons to build a palatial residence eventually known as Castle in the Clouds. The incredible work of these artisans is apparent everywhere on this property. For instance, to the left of the Falls Footpath, field-stone stairs wind up the steep embankment of the ravine and through the woods in the direction of the falls. Guests at the estate no doubt took this idyllic woodland shortcut from the grounds above to the base of the waterfall.

Now, a picnic table has been placed conveniently beneath the shade of a graceful copse of white paper birches.

The Falls of Song at Castle Springs.

At the beginning of a boardwalk palisade leading to the foot of the cascade, look to your right at eye level and you'll see the smooth green-and-white trunk of a striped maple. This understory tree may be identified by its three-toed, webfoot-shaped leaves. For this reason it has been nicknamed goosefoot maple. If you aren't satisfied with these names, try moosewood maple, after the moose that nibble the foliage of this common New Hampshire tree.

Specimens of mountain maple also are found here, to the left growing out of the embankment wall. Mountain maples characteristically grow no larger than bushes, and feature maple-shaped leaves.

Walk about 200 feet on the boardwalk to the lookout platform. The falls spill 50 feet from the clifftop above to the pool below. The thunderous pounding of the water sounds more like an anvil chorus than a "song," but along with the mist, it definitely adds to the spectacle.

The magically clear wishing-well pool at the base of the falls casts a spell over visitors, and bright pennies shine below the moss-covered rocks. (Please refrain from this gesture yourself, since the copper pennies can harm wildlife.) At the water's edge the moist, graceful fronds of shield ferns dip and sway in the spray. Although on the short side, this trail has a dramatic climax likely to please all ages.

If you continue up the access road and park at the main lot, you will see a number of landscaped plants. Heart-shaped leaves twining up the trunks belong to a woody vine called Dutchman's-pipe. On an embankment over the parking area in spring the lovely rose-colored flowers of bristly locust (a shrub related to black locust) droop from round-leaved fronds. Other ornamentals include ginkgo trees with their fan-shaped yellow leaves, Virginia creeper, lilacs, and forsythia.

Getting There

From NH 25 (east of Moultonborough) turn south onto NH 109 and drive 2.2 miles. Continue south on NH 171 for 2.1 miles. Turn left at Castle Springs Main Entrance Road. From the gate/tollhouse the Falls Footpath is at 0.4 mile on the right. (Look for the sign.)

Other Information

Castle Springs
P.O. Box 131, Route 171
Moultonborough, NH 03254
603-476-2352

Open daily June 15 through Labor Day. General grounds fee required (less than for the Castle in the Clouds tour). You can tour the castle and visit the Castle Springs bottling plant on the same grounds. Three other blazed trails range from less than a mile to the twelve-mile Faraway Trail, with a view of Lake Winnipesaukee.

Castle Springs
Trout Pond Trail (Loop)
Moultonborough

- **0.75 mile**
- **20 minutes**
- **easy**

A country fish pond with many birds and a feeding platform to watch lunker trout perform for a handful of food.

Imagine how this property looked in 1913 when retired manufacturer Thomas Plant built his palatial residence on the top of 2,215-foot Bald Peak. He stabled horses at the south end of the pond and hired workers to maintain thirty miles of bridle trails. During work on a nine-hole golf course (no longer here), a family cemetery plot was discovered. Mr. Plant was about to remove the gravestones and coffins when the Carroll County sheriff stepped in. Plant was forced to leave the cemetery intact.

Shannon Pond, created from water diverted from Shannon Brook, was designed for anglers to practice their fly-fishing skills. The nearby golf course was kept clipped by a herd of sheep imported from Scotland. Eventually, Plant turned the estate grounds into an exclusive private club for influential guests and friends.

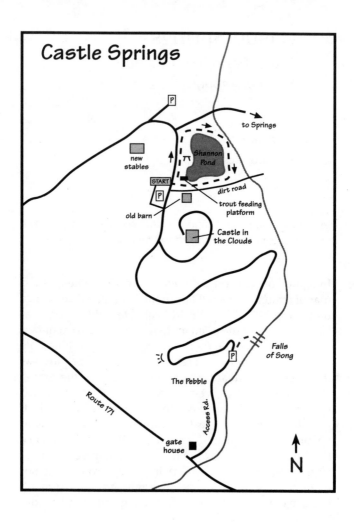

Castle Springs

P

to Springs

new
stables

START

Shannon
Pond

P

old barn

dirt road

trout feeding
platform

Castle in
the Clouds

Falls
of Song

P

The Pebble

Route 171

Access Rd.

gate
house

N

Across from the parking area and main road is a covered kiosk giving trail information. A hexagonal orange metal blaze with a white arrow affixed to the signboard points left. Walk the road toward the new barn on the hill. Picnic tables and Shannon Pond are on the right.

At the north end of the pond a woods road with a gate and sign reading No Unauthorized Vehicles leads to the spring source of Castle Springs bottled water.

Turn right on this road. Note the clump of paper birches at this end of the pond. Paper birch is also called canoe birch because Native Americans used the smooth waterproof bark on the outside of their canoes.

Many tribes were present in the region when white men arrived. The Sokoki tribe lived on the northeastern end of Lake Winnipesaukee. The Ossipee tribe camped at Lake Ossipee to the east of these mountains, and the Penacooks summered on the south end of Lake Winnipesaukee. All of these tribes were a part of the Penacook Confederacy, which was a sort of United Nations of eastern seaboard tribes.

Centuries before this land was turned into a playground for the wealthy, these various tribes kept to the high ground, traveling footpaths along eskers and ridges from lake to lake. Frequently, they met in what is now Moultonborough to trade. In spring they caught and cured the salmon that spawned and ran in the streams and falls like those on this property.

The pond inlet burbles through a stone viaduct into the pond. Some of the 1,000 Italian masons hired to build the Plant mansion also built bridges, kennels, and stone retaining walls. Much of the masonry still is functioning and in plain sight.

At 0.2 mile follow the orange blaze and turn right into the woods. (A word of caution: This trail doubles as a bridle path. It can be muddy and full of horse "chestnuts" that don't come from a tree. Watch your step.) This eastern side of the pond is forested with tall white pine. White pine have straight black trunks and long needles that grow in groups of five. If the needles are too far up in the canopy, look on the ground for the five-to-six-inch-long and narrow pine cones.

Ostrich ferns, which grow to five feet tall, may be identified by their fronds, which form a tapered plume.

Trout-feeding platform at Castle Springs.

The tiny basal leaves gradually widen about three feet up the stipe (central stalk) and then taper again at the end.

By 0.3 mile (no blaze) you're already at the dirt road leading a short distance back to the brown barn. Turn right. Barn swallows (blue-black above and tan underneath, with a true "swallowtail") swoop overhead. Brown-and-white striped song sparrows also make this country meadow their home, and you may hear their sweet, clear high song. They are identified by a dark spot below their white chortling throats.

At about 0.4 mile walk down to a platform that juts over the pond. Feeding dispensers have been placed on the edge of the railing. For a quarter a handful you may feed the fish. The trout are clearly visible and perpetually hungry. Several lunkers (overgrown trophy fish) look like they haven't stopped eating since Thomas Plant first stocked the pond.

If you have followed the Castle Springs map picked up at the gatehouse, you will realize that the distance you have walked around the pond doesn't coincide with the mileage indicated. Other hiking trails listed on this map include Oak Ridge, Bald Knob, and Mount Faraway.

Getting There

From NH 25 (east of Moultonborough) turn south onto NH 109 and drive 2.2 miles. Continue south on NH 171 for 2.1 miles. Turn left at Castle Springs Main Entrance Road. Drive the access road (nearly 2 miles) to a sign reading Stables. Main parking is to the right of this road at the top of the hill—but don't park here. Descend toward a field with a pond on the right. Park on the left under a clump of oaks. The pond hiking kiosk and covered picnic tables are to the right.

Other Information

Castle Springs
P.O. Box 131 Route 171
Moultonborough, NH 03254
603-476-2352

Open weekends and holidays from May 11, daily from June 15 through Labor Day; hours: 9:00 A.M. to 5:00 P.M. Labor Day through October 19; hours 9:00 A.M. to 4:00 P.M. General Admission and castle tour fees. Call for details.

Frederick & Paula Anna Markus Audubon Wildlife Sanctuary

Loon Nest Trail
Moultonborough

- **1.6 miles**
- **1 hour**
- **moderate**

On a far northeast inlet of Lake Winnipesaukee, a pair of nesting loons provide the focus for public awareness and this trail behind the new Loon Center headquarters.

Loons have good press in New Hampshire, maybe because of the haunting cry of the loons in the movie *On Golden Pond*, filmed on Squam Lake. Artists and photographers also keep loons in the public eye, as seen by the items in the gift shop at the new Loon Center.

Stop here first and ask a staff member to play one of their videos. In all probability, this will be the closest you'll come to a nesting loon unless you have a canoe or kayak. The pair of nesting loons on this property is well hidden in tall marsh grass. However, the exhibits and video orient visitors so that they know what to watch and listen for as they walk the trail.

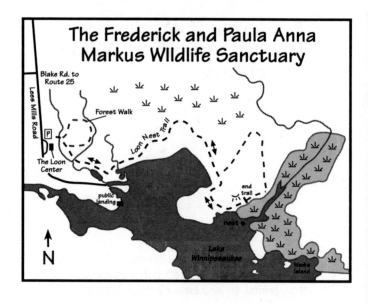

The Frederick and Paula Anna
Markus Wildlife Sanctuary

Once endangered in Vermont, and with dwindling populations in other New England states, the good news is that the 65-million-year-old common loon has made a strong and successful comeback. And this bears testimony to efforts like those of the Loon Preservation Committee and Educational Center.

Loons reclaim the same nests year after year. Both parents share the hatching, turning over two to three bronze-colored eggs with their bills as they take turns on the nest. For four weeks they occupy a hummock of grass molded into a nest, watching for predatory beaver and turtles and assiduously tending the eggs. Chicks are charcoal colored and ride piggyback (well, loonback) until they're old enough to swim and dive for frogs, crayfish, plant roots, and other delectables in their diet.

At the center you also learn some disconcerting facts about the battle facing the Loon Preservation Committee. Fortunately, plastic six-pack carrying cases are banned in many states. But toxic lead fishing sinkers still are sold and cause the mortality of hundreds of loons and other water birds each year. Invisible hydrocarbon, sulfur, and nitrogen oxide emissions have a slow but deleterious effect on northern lakes. Logging and paper-mill chemicals create another long-standing problem in this and other regions of New England.

An understanding of the delicate balance between the private life of the loon and infringements of man enhances the walk to the nesting site. The trailhead starts to the right of the center as you face the building. At the outset follow a rock-bordered path. Before crossing a new bridge over Halfway Brook, pick up a trail flier. Although the Audubon map indicates two "vantage points," the first one is closer and is the destination on our walk.

Cross several log footbridges through a muddy slough overgrown with wide, scalloped sensitive ferns (sensitive because they die at the first hint of frost in fall) and four-foot-tall cinnamon ferns (so called because their spores are attached to a separate stalk which in late spring turns brown as a cinnamon stick).

At 0.2 mile cross a bridge and marshy area to the left. After another 0.1 mile, the terrain changes. Sugar maples and granite boulders now line the path, sometimes spilling into it. The inlet at 0.6 mile presents the best opening of this Winnipesaukee cove. The marsh

Thanks to active preservation groups, loons are making a comeback on New Hampshire lakes and ponds.

where the loon nest is located is to the left as you face the water.

The flier warns walkers to "beware of ticks in grassy areas." Most of this trail (a loop) is a grassy area, infested with ticks and mosquitoes. Being aware of them, unlike learning about the loons, doesn't make one sympathetic to their existence.

This is the reason we recommend stopping at the first vantage point. Climb up a forested hillock. Children will enjoy the passage between two huge boulders, as well as the name for the lichen growing on them—"rock tripe," because they resemble tripe.

At 0.8 mile to the right is the marsh where supposedly you can see the loon nest. If you don't, there's still plenty to contemplate in this extensive backwater. Red-winged blackbirds click and screech in the tall reeds and cattails where they make their home. Such decidedly "undeveloped" land as this has a wide variety of wildlife eating and being eaten. Flycatchers, bats, frogs, fish, and dragonflies go after mosquitoes, and there are plenty to go around. Great blue heron, ducks, and loons go after the frogs and smaller fish. And so it goes, up the food chain.

After surveying the marsh, we suggest you return the way you came, stopping for a last look at the lakeside. Elsewhere in the past, one of us was swimming in a similar cove and was surprised to look into the curious red eye of a loon 20 feet away focused on her red swimming cap. However, most loons don't get that close; they dive and swim underwater (up to 200 feet), often emerging at a safer distance in the middle of the lake.

CHICKS STATISTICS

From Squam, Winnipesaukee, Massabesic, and Umbagog Lakes*

Total Loon Population	594
Loon Couples from 201 Territories	402
Loon Nests	122
Pairs with Chicks (65% successful)	79
Chicks Hatched	115
Chicks Living at End of Season	84

* For 1995

Getting There

From NH 25 on the west side of Moultonborough at Central High School, turn left onto Blake Road (there is a Loon Center sign on NH 25 opposite Blake Road). Drive 0.5 mile. Here Blake Road turns from asphalt to hard-packed dirt. At 1.0 mile turn right onto Lees Mill Road. Drive 0.2 mile; the Loon Center and parking lot are on the left.

Affiliated Organizations

Audubon Society of New Hampshire
3 Silk Road
Concord, NH 03301
603-476-LOON

Alice Bemis Thompson Audubon Bird Sanctuary and Wildlife Refuge

Old Lane Marsh Trail

North Sandwich

- **0.6 mile**
- **30 minutes**
- **easy**

Spectacular sweeping views of mountain ranges from the midst of a bird-filled marsh.

This trail hides a surprise. At first the short, flat walk shows no prospect of long-range scenes. But once you're past the tree-lined road, the old lane turns into a footpath through reed and rush grasses. By the time you reach the footbridge across Atwood Brook the sky vault opens and your eyes reach to the long horizons.

After entering the wide pathway at the trailhead, look for an Audubon Society guidebook in a mailbox on the right. On the way down the old road watch for soft-needled firs growing along the trail, mountain laurels (the baby siblings of rhododendron, both of which are members of the heath family), and, most striking of all, American larches, or tamaracks.

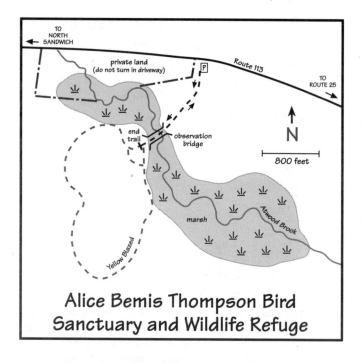

Alice Bemis Thompson Bird
Sanctuary and Wildlife Refuge

Tamaracks are unique, the only conifer (cone-bearing) tree that sheds all its needles in the fall. In season silky dark needles grow in tufts directly from the branches and not from the ends of twigs. Tamaracks have a science-fiction quality to them, with their rough bark often draped with aerial mosses or scaled with lichen. They grow near bogs and marshes.

To the right of the lane the marsh is partially veiled by a tangled tree-and-shrub border. As the trail curves right ahead, the open light of the marsh shines through from the left.

Suddenly, at 0.1 mile from the trailhead, the marsh appears in broad view while the trail narrows and leads you over a gravel pathway through pliant waist-high marsh grass. The grass bends over the trail as you sweep through it, forcing your eyes to your boots to keep steady footing.

Then, again suddenly, at 0.2 mile you reach the sturdy plank footbridge over Atwood Brook. Now you can stand without keeping an eye on your footsteps and gasp at the far horizons before and behind you.

To the southeast lie the Ossipee Mountains—from left to right: Bald Mountain, Larcom Mountain, Johnson Mountain, and Black Snout. To the northwest are seven peaks, including Sandwich Mountain, Whiteface, Mount Paugus, and, most famous of all, Mount Chocorua.

Beaver are latecomers to this area—the marsh used to be a meadow. The Joseph Corliss family arrived here in the early nineteenth century. Later generations turned the former meadow into a hayfield for farming. Joseph's son, Benjamin, and then Benjamin's son, Hiram, kept farming the hay. The last generation gave us famed "Corliss baskets," hand split and woven from brown ash.

Charles Thompson of South Tamworth took ownership of the land and eventually deeded 172 acres of it to the Audubon Society in 1977. Two years later Frank and Rose Church added 66 adjacent acres for more protection.

A painted turtle crawls on the Old Lane Marsh Trail.

The marsh is replete with wildlife of all sorts, water-loving birds especially—great blue heron, kingfishers, ducks, red-winged blackbirds, flycatchers. Take time to look in the reeds. Be patient and aware of movement, color, distinct sounds. Frogs, crayfish, salamanders, and newts ply the waters while moose, white-tailed deer, and black bear have been sighted on the periphery of the forest that surrounds the vast marsh.

Continue another 0.1 mile from the bridge to the other edge of the marsh and proceed into the trees. This gives you a sense of the surrounding effect of the woods on both sides of the marsh.

However, when you see the junction of the yellow-blazed long loop trail with the red-blazed short loop, consider stopping and turning around to head back. The yellow-blazed trail for us entailed several bypasses around downed trees. One fallen giant had the metal yellow blaze dangling from its supine girth without a clue to the direction of the trail. Unless recent trail maintenance seems obvious at the outset, it's better to forgo this longer loop and savor the early splendors of the marsh.

Getting There

From NH 25 at Bennett Corner with a sign to Covered Bridge No. 45, turn onto NH 113 toward North Sandwich. Drive 2.8 miles and park on the left at the Audubon sign and gate.

Affiliated Organizations

Audubon Society of New Hampshire
3 Silk Road
Concord, NH 03301
603-224-9909

White Lake State Park
White Lake & Pitch Pines Trail (Loop)
Tamworth/West Ossipee

- **2.4 miles**
- **1 hour**
- **easy**

> *The great blue heron*
> *glides behind a scrim of reeds*
> *like the old man in Shakespeare about his dark deeds.*
> *We move without thinking; he thinks without blinking.*
> *From the shore a shadow blurs, recedes.*
> -J.O.

Well-maintained trails, forest biodiversity, and a mirrored view in clear lake water blend in this harmonious outing. The trailhead begins opposite the parking area to the left of the large swimming beach (as you face the lake).

Twenty-five feet beyond a picturesque footbridge paralleling the shore are two clumps of gray birch with light gray trunks and sharply pointed triangular leaves. Pass between them and you're on the trail. There are no blazes but the flat pine-needle path is well defined and easy to follow.

Whereas southerners look forward to wild azaleas and rhododendrons in the spring, northern New Englan-

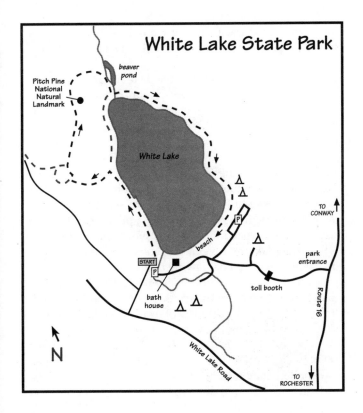

White Lake State Park

Pitch Pine National Natural Landmark

beaver pond

White Lake

TO CONWAY

park entrance

toll booth

Route 16

beach

START

bath house

White Lake Road

TO ROCHESTER

N

ders patiently await the pink and white clusters of mountain laurel. Mountain laurel, an acid-loving member of the heath family, often is found in conjunction with conifers, whose needles add acid to the soil. It is right at home here with the pitch pines. Each individual flower, shaped like a tiny saucer, catches and absorbs some of the spring rain. When the seasonal extravaganza of the laurel fades, next to them the white bell-like flowers of lowbush blueberries bloom, eventually turning to the dark wine-flavored fruit.

Along the shallows of the lake is arrowhead, a water-loving plant with arrow-shaped narrow leaves and white blossoms. The Penacook Indians living in this region ate the roots of these and other freshwater aquatic plants.

After half a mile, the Pitch Pine Trail loop comes in from the left, hooking up with the White Lake Trail loop. Turn left at the white blazes onto the Pitch Pine Trail. A good way to identify these trees is to see if the needles are growing in groups of three (like a pitchfork). The stiff needles are twisted and show white pores through which they take in oxygen. But most probably the needles will be well out of viewing range, since mature pitch pines like these grow up to seventy feet high. The reddish furrowed bark of the trunk can lend another identification clue—sticky droplets of resin or pitch. Avoid getting this on your hands; it doesn't come off easily.

The sex life of the pitch pine takes off when the tree is about eight years old. Male flowers emit clouds of yellow pollen that fertilize female gumdrop-sized cones growing on the same tree. Mature cones are stubby and stalkless, with sharp thorned tips that protect the seeds inside. In fact, they're so well protected often the seeds never are released. Trees displaying this kind of delayed seed release are known as *serotinous* trees, and foresters recommend turning on the heat to solve the problem. Whereas most trees are vulnerable to forest fires, pitch pines actually profit from "controlled burns." They not only release seeds, but the clearing of the understory produces the perfect environment for pitch-pine seedlings to grow in the sun. This seventy-two-acre stand of mature pitch pine at White Lake State Park has been set aside as a Natural Landmark.

Settlers in the northern provinces tapped trees like these in the same way they tapped maples. The pitch they collected had a variety of uses. The resin was used in the waterproofing of boats, and the pine knots were fashioned into torches because the pitch burned so brightly. "Candlewood" was a nickname for this multi-use tree. Native New England red pine resembles pitch pine but grows twenty feet taller, reseeds more easily, and produces a higher grade of lumber.

An informative brochure about this stand of pitch pine suggests that you listen for the one-note musical

Ducklings at White Lake State Park.

trill of the pine warbler. And it is true that you probably will hear this warbler high in the canopy. The olive-yellow small bird doesn't migrate too far south and often stops at New Hampshire feeders late in winter. Where there are pines, you'll often see or hear this warbler.

At 0.7 mile turn away from the marsh on your left. Bear, raccoon and other animals living within White Lake State Park may be seen on this walk in the twilight or early dawn, but during the day the mosquito reigns supreme and keeps walkers moving. At 0.8 mile turn right at the Pitch Pine Trail sign and follow the white blazes back through the forest to the lake shore at 1.3 miles.

The Pitch Pine spur loop reunites with the larger White Lake loop on a backwater formed by beaver activity downstream. When we were there, two great blue heron were searching for frogs, crawdads, small freshwater clams, and other delicacies in this standing pool. A chance encounter with a great blue heron can startle both of you. Nose to beak, they can stretch their long necks to equal human stature—and freeze you in your tracks with their yellow eyes.

At 1.4 miles cross a footbridge over another backwater dark with tannin from the rotting trees. A tepee-shaped beaver house is just one of many visible signs indicating the presence of this large member of the rodent family. Beaver have whittled many trees on the lake shore and along the trail. Like loggers, first they saw the trunk with their sharp front teeth. Then they munch on the leaves. Next, they drag or float the defoliated limbs to their house site. The busy beavers target larger trees to construct a dam across tributaries and inlets, thus creating private pools ideal for raising their families.

At 1.5 miles a mammoth maple and a whopping tall white pine hug the trail to your left. One more footbridge and you're back on the edge of the lake.

At 1.8 miles the foothills of the White Mountains and the distinctive pointed peak of Chocorua are reflected in the mirrored surface of the limpid lake water. But keep vigilant because the trail here is riddled with tree roots.

At 2.0 miles veer away from the shoreline and into the woods. Cross a footbridge, and in a short distance the trail suddenly ends at campsite 13 of the campground. Our walk continues on the dirt road along the lake to the right (campsites 13-1). At campsite 1 turn off the dirt road and to the right. You'll pass campsite 3 on your left. Continue on a worn path between two posts to the swimming beach and picnic area at 2.3 miles.

Here you can relax and enjoy the view before continuing along the shore to your starting point.

Getting There

From the junction of NH 25 and NH 16 in West Ossipee, drive north on NH 16 for 0.5 mile. White Lake State Park is on the left. From the park toll booth drive 0.2 mile to Beach Parking (the sign Store points to the right). Turn left onto an asphalt road marked Dead End. Pass the Bath House on your right. Park to the left at the end of the road.

Other Information

White Lake State Park
Box 41
West Ossipee, NH 03890
603-323-7350

Science Center of New Hampshire

Gephart Exhibit Trail (Loop)

Holderness

- **1 mile**
- **1 hour and 30 minutes**
- **easy**

---

*A wonderful stroll for families to see and learn
about black bear, bald eagles, bobcats, great horned owls,
and many other examples of large and small wildlife
displayed and explained in naturalistic enclosures.*

Although this trail is more zoolike than woodsy, you do have the opportunity to see native New Hampshire wildlife up close—and this is special because the chances of seeing wary bobcats and majestic bald eagles a few feet away in the wild are slim.

The name Science Center may mislead some people. As a fenced-in outdoor wildlife museum, the center offers an educational walk among creatures of land and air. The animals and birds here are too injured or medically disabled to survive in the wilderness.

The trail begins at the main building of the center. Visitors exit the back door and pass a sign: The Gephart

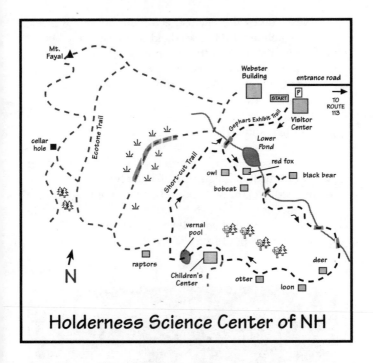

Holderness Science Center of NH

Trail in memory of William Stephen Gephart 1951–1968.

Once outside, follow the well-maintained trail through the grounds. Turn left at a log lectern in front of a bank of benches for tour groups and special programs.

The rock-lined path curves and winds through lush woods. You'll learn at the first exhibit how a red fox redesigns old woodchuck burrows for its own family den and how fox hunt for small mammals, bird eggs, insects, and berries.

Next comes the enclosure for the bobcat. A sleek, prowling feline with black-edged white ears, the bobcat is among the most efficient predators in the forest. Unusual for a feline, it hunts in trees as well as on the ground. Once it catches its prey, it may store what it doesn't eat in caches.

Circle by a pond again, cross the bridge over the pond outlet, and arrive at a cage of American black bear, a species which can weigh in when mature at 600 pounds. They're fast on their feet and furious with their jaws—but most of all shy. In 1977 the female at the center arrived weighing 8 pounds and suffering from a brain infection (fortunately she recovered). An eight-month-old male arrived in 1995 and will reach full maturity when he's about five years old.

Bald eagles see eye to eye.

Be sure to explore the fascinating information in the shed across from the bears. The exhibit has question-and-answer boards set up to tantalize young people. The truth is that, yes, bears do have a sweet tooth for the honey found in beehives. Every day they eat 11–18 pounds of food. Black bear have increased in number to about 3,000 in New Hampshire and have expanded their range. If you're anxious about bears in the woods, one way to keep these shy, roaming animals away is to make some noise as you walk along by talking normally or whistling or rattling a stone in an empty can.

Proceed down and around the slopes as the trail curves around the bear cage. Turn right again before approaching the next hillside enclosure for white-tailed deer and wild turkey. The wild turkey, which had dwindled in numbers, was reintroduced to the New Hampshire woods a few decades ago. They are alive and well: last fall we spotted a dozen females waddling through a ravine with Tom at the rear.

Within sight of the shed, Turtle Island displays snapping turtles, painted turtles, and many other species.

As the trail moves upward, the loon shed to the left nearby displays a "Loon Menu," including frogs, crayfish, plant roots, sunfish, perch, minnows, and other delectables. This diet allows loons to live twenty to thirty years, fly 60 MPH, dive 200 feet, and weigh 6.5–8.5 pounds. The loon population in New Hampshire, once very seriously threatened, now totals 557, a measure of success in bringing back these intriguing birds.

Children will be entranced by the river otter gliding through the water and over the rockslide of its natural-looking enclosure. (River otters in the wild need up to thirty miles of territory for food foraging to survive.)

Looking through the glass wall, you can see its whiskers for detecting prey in murky water, its webbed feet for swift swimming, dense underfur for warmth and waterproofing, and long tail used as a rudder in water and for propping itself upright on land. Walk around the glass wall to another window below to the right, where you can see the otter speeding underwater.

Next on the trail as it loops into the woods again comes the bird museum, where you learn to tell what food birds eat by the shape of their beaks and feet (fat beaks to crack seeds, long legs to hunt frogs and fish in shoreline water). Eggs are described as "packages of inheritance" and are explained in detail.

Children will enjoy the next large shed with a rope spider web, a spiral staircase in a two-story treehouse, a groundhog tunnel to explore, and other appealing play adventures.

Then the trail takes you to a view of what lies underground. Microscopes are set up, and through a lens you can inspect a handful of plain old dirt. It contains 1 billion protozoa, 30,000 nematodes, 2,000 mites, 100 insects, two earthworms, and other creatures—an amazing profusion of life on earth.

Here, too, you'll discover that a shrew, even though it weighs only two ounces, eats 50 percent of its body weight every day. Translate this into human equivalents: a 118-pound woman would have to eat 59 pounds of food a day to match the habits of the shrew. Of course, humans don't need that much food. It's the shrew's speedy metabolism that requires such consumption.

A great horned owl shakes out his feathers when we shake out our collapsible red umbrella.

In the raptor section, a member of the largest owl family in New Hampshire—the great horned owl—keeps an august, penetrating eye on visitors. This night predator uses the soft feathers of its three-to-five-foot wing span for silent gliding after prey (it can locate a mouse seventy-five feet away). The black-and-white night vision of the great horned owl is 100 times more acute than ours.

The red-tailed hawk has color vision eight times better than humans' for its daylight hunts.

In the next enclosure, two commanding bald eagles, our national bird, bring the power of their beaks and claws and their six-to-seven-foot wingspans into perspective when seen so close, instead of watching them circle hundreds of feet above.

Follow the arrows back to the main building and leave the center with vivid memories of this engrossing wildlife walk.

Getting There

In the center of Holderness where the Holderness Public Library is located, turn onto NH 113 at the junction of NH 25 and US 3. In 0.2 mile turn left at the Science Center sign and drive 0.2 mile up the access road to the parking lot.

Other Information

Science Center of New Hampshire
P.O. Box 173
Holderness, NH 03245
603-968-7194

Hours: Exhibit season May 1 to November 1, 9:30 A.M. to 4:30 P.M. daily (last admission at 3:30 P.M.).

Science Center of New Hampshire

Ecotone & Mount Fayal Summit Trails (Loop)

Holderness

- **1.4 miles**
- **1 hour and 15 minutes**
- **moderately difficult (good climb)**

After a meadow stroll, the walk ascends a well-designed, well-maintained trail through spacious woods to the 1,067-foot summit of Mount Fayal and a wonderful view overlooking the cove-etched shore of Squam Lake.

Combining part of the Ecotone Trail with the Mount Fayal Summit Trail gives you the best of two worlds—a wildflower-packed meadow with a sumptuous lake view typifying this area of the state.

Proceed onto the mowed-grass Ecotone Trail (an ecotone is an "edge" border between natural communities; it's usually identified as a forest-field ecotone exactly like the one you're walking). To the left, as you skirt the high side of the field, the grassy terrain slants down toward the wildlife exhibit area of the Science Center. To the right, the forested base of Mount Fayal slants toward the summit. In midsummer as you walk the first half of

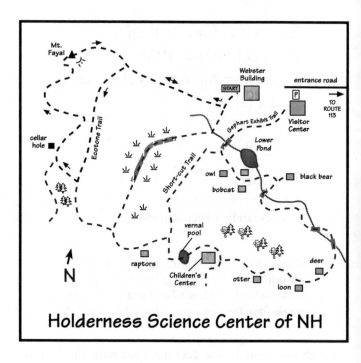

Holderness Science Center of NH

the Ecotone Trail, plant life abounds—yarrow, milk-weed, black-eyed Susans, vetch, clover, and many grass-es and other blossoms.

Milkweed acts as a host plant to butterflies. In July and August you'll see these exotic winged insects flut-tering from one nectar-bearing pink flower cluster to the next. Monarchs especially are attracted to milkweed and obtain an interesting form of protection from the plant. First, they lay their eggs on the underside of the leaves. Caterpillars hatch and eat the nourishing milkweed leaves, which contain a cardiac glycoside, a highly distasteful toxin that is stored in the caterpillars' abdomens. The caterpillars retain the toxin through the butterfly stage. Birds come to realize that the rust-colored, large monarchs taste awful and can, in fact, cause vomiting. Thus the milkweed renders the butterfly inedible to predators.

In 300 feet the trail enters the woods where a wild apple tree grows on the right, a speckled alder shrub on the left.

In another 100 feet a Y junction marks the Mount Fayal Summit Trail to the right and the Ecotone Trail to the left. Go to the left (the Mount Fayal Trail at this point leads up a much steeper climb).

As you continue along the Ecotone Trail in the bordering woods now, notice the identified trees along the way—witch hazel, gray birch, hemlock, red maple, and hop hornbeam with its small serrated leaf. This makes an up-close, hands-on classroom for tree identification.

The trail curves in a wide arc through the woods as it moves around the field toward the left. At this point the Ecotone Trail crosses two footbridges a short distance from each other. The second bridge lies near wild grapes growing plentifully in their favored location close to water.

At 0.2 mile from the trailhead, reenter the top edge of the meadow with daisies, asters, and birdhouses scattered around. This type of setting provides ample food, shelter, and space for a variety of wildlife.

At 0.21 mile a Y junction with a grove of staghorn sumac to the left marks the trailhead to the Mount Fayal Summit Trail on the right. Sumac trees are shaped like tall umbrellas. The trunks are upright, yet flexible. The "staghorn" name comes from its branches, which

White Admiral butterfly.

appeared to be covered with a fuzzy coating, as antelope antlers are when newly grown. The sumac produces burgundy-colored, cone-shaped, fuzzy fruits in the fall that are high in vitamin C and are a favorite of birds.

Now the walk shifts into a climbing mode as you ascend a wide trail through mixed woods of deciduous oak and maple among the evergreen, white pine, and hemlock.

The first fifty feet of this orange-dot-blazed pathway are laid out as a kind of "corduroy trail" with logs laid lengthwise to each other as a means of securing the topsoil against water erosion.

At 0.34 mile cross a small brook flowing from the left. As you proceed up the rocky trail, a needle path soon takes over. Needles mean evergreens. We've discovered that pine and fir forests seem to host fewer mosquitoes—perhaps because the needle path dries faster. Mosquito larvae require water, and leaf mulch from the deciduous trees retains moisture, creating vernal pools early in the season.

At nearly a half-mile from the Ecotone trailhead, the Mount Fayal Summit Trail levels. Ahead, a sign to the left explains that the land here used to be the Piper Homestead. Occupied by James Piper, his wife, Saphronia, and their four children from 1840 to 1890, the homestead flourished until the farmhouse burned down. The farm at the time grew wheat, corn, oats, hay, potatoes, peas and beans, and produced maple sugar and butter. A cellar hole remains of the Piper Homestead to the left.

From this site, proceed straight ahead (not onto the trail to the left). The first part of the next section lies relatively level in airy woods, and, although the trail is wide, tree roots abound underfoot.

Gradually ascend through many pines. The closer to the summit, the more the woods thin, allowing you to see farther into the forest on both sides.

Suddenly at 0.74 mile, a hairpin turn on an ascending part of the trail takes you to the summit with a sign reading Mount Fayal 1,067'. The top of the mountain returns to mixed woods, mostly oak and white pine.

A natural reaction at reaching a summit is to stop, rest, and see what's to see. Instead, continue another 100 feet on the trail down to the main view—a spectacular long and narrow corridor cut through the woods overlooking Squam Lake. The ragged shoreline of the tree-lined lake curves in and out, angling and narrowing the deep blue water quilt to the left into the rich green woodlands. This is a mountaintop memory you'll keep a long time.

The remainder of the loop walk descends the mountainside on a well-structured pathway with occasional log railings for handholds, drainage ditches, and secure footsteps. The descent is steep in some sections, but the entire route is manageable for nearly anyone.

The trail passes through deciduous woods, crosses a log road at 1.19 miles and returns to hemlock and white-pine groves—nice needle paths again.

At 1.27 miles cross a footbridge to the Y junction with the Ecotone Trail (the junction at the outset of the walk).

At the junction, take the left fork to the Webster Building at 1.32 miles and the visitor center at 1.37 miles.

Getting There

In the center of Holderness where the Holderness Public Library is located, turn onto NH 113 at the junction of NH 25 and US 3. In 0.2 mile turn left at the Science Center sign and drive 0.2 mile up the access road to the parking lot. To reach the trailhead, walk through the wide porch of the Webster Building at the right of the main entrance and toward the edge of the meadow where a post marker reads Exhibit Trail and Ecotone Trail.

Other Information

Science Center of New Hampshire
P.O. Box 173
Holderness, NH 03245
603-968-7194

Trail hours: May through October, admission desk open daily 9:30 A.M. to 3:30 P.M. The center closes at 4:30 P.M.

Madison Boulder State Wayside: A Geological Park

Boulder Trail (Loop)

Madison

- **0.2 mile**
- **15 minutes**
- **easy**

---

*A walk encircling one of the largest
glacial erratics in the world.*

This is a short walk, but it takes you to an extraordinary sight: an enormous boulder, a glacial erratic that was deposited here during the Ice Age. The boulder—87 feet long, 23 feet wide, 37 feet high, and weighing an esti-mated 4,662 tons—and surrounding land were given to the state in 1946 in memory of James O. Gerry and A. Crosby Kennett.

The path circling the boulder begins in plain sight at the end of the parking area. The rock isn't far away, and believe us, you can't miss it.

New England's glacial erratics are stones of any size that were carried, pushed, or otherwise moved by the colossal force of the glaciers. They are called "erratic" because their geologic structure often doesn't match the nearby rock. The Madison Boulder was dragged here by

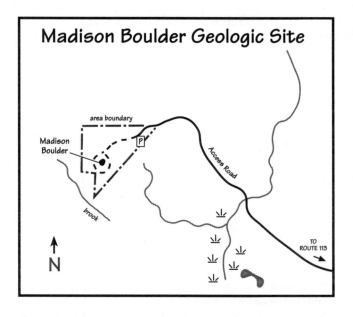

Madison Boulder Geologic Site

area boundary

Madison
Boulder

P

Access Road

brook

N

TO
ROUTE 113

the one-mile-thick, continent-wide glacier that covered
much of eastern North America 25,000 years ago. The
glacier crept down from the north, dragging this and
millions of other rocks along in its bulk. Some
12,000–10,000 years ago the climate warmed and the
glacier melted; this boulder and its traveling companions simply settled down where they were—which is
one reason why New England is such a stony locale.

The glaciers were astounding in size—thick enough
to cover the White Mountains. They were so heavy that
they depressed the continental land mass with their

weight. When the glaciers finally melted and retreated, they left behind not only stones but also depressions that helped to create the hundreds of lakes that now dot this region of New Hampshire.

Louis Agassiz, the Swiss-born luminary of nineteenth-century science who taught at Harvard for many years, is credited with developing theories about the Ice Age. Some erratics were carried hundreds of miles but others came from much nearer their final destination: experts calculate that Madison Boulder was pushed to its present location from about two miles north.

Of course, the boulder isn't the only bit of nature here. On your circuit around the boulder take a look at the plant life in the surrounding woods. The white pine

Madison Boulder–a glacial erratic deposited here during the Ice Ages.

and hemlock are healthy and handsome here. Look for interrupted ferns, which you can identify by the fronds in each cluster that are "interrupted" halfway up the stalks by dried, brown clusters of seed sacs. Behind the boulder, a small brook gurgles in spring and early summer straight down the hillside.

At the back, too, notice a tall tree trunk with shaggy bark. On first sight this may appear to be a shagbark hickory, but it's really a mature, tall red maple. Older maple bark curls out as the years accumulate (although this process isn't as pronounced as with shagbark hickories).

Walking to the other side of the boulder and back toward the parking area, watch for a series of small disklike, gray-brown lichen known as rock tripe clinging tightly to smaller boulders in the area. These are attached to the rock by tiny rhizomes (thin rooting strands). Lichen is interesting; not really a single plant, it is a symbiotic association of fungi and green algae. It survives through the photosynthesizing nourishment of algae that grow beneath the lichen "disks."

Getting There

From the center of Madison, drive north on NH 113 2.1 miles to a sign that reads Madison Boulder Next Left. Turn left and drive 0.9 mile to the access road to the geological park. Drive 0.4 mile more to the parking lot.

West

Rollins State Park
Mount Kearsarge Summit Trail
Warner

- **1.4 miles**
- **1 hour**
- **easy ascent**

A wide, well-developed mountain trail to a 2,917-foot bald summit with sensational full-circle views.

The 3.5-mile drive up the southern side of Mount Kearsarge offers a wonderful introduction to this walk. The asphalt auto road is a pleasant, narrow ascent that passes through picnic areas, by high overlooks, and alongside tall birch, oak, and many other hardwoods. At 1.2 miles from the ranger tollgate, the road levels and the trees thin to spruce and hemlock. In another half-mile, Black Mountain appears from the first turnout to the west.

Another turnout comes up at 2.3 miles on the right with an outstanding view of Little Mountain to the southeast. Go 0.1 mile more and you'll see layer upon layer of mountains falling away to the green-blue horizons. A

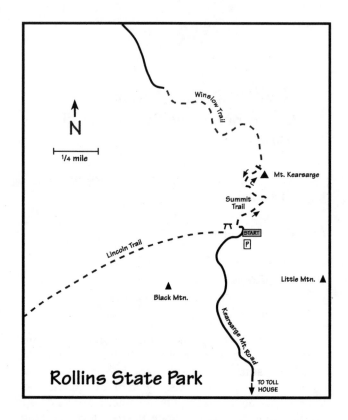

Rollins State Park

small alcove picnic site beside a brook awaits 0.2 mile farther.

At 3.2 miles from the entrance gate, a turnout on the left gives you another sweeping view to the east—Mount Sunapee, the town of New London, Prescott Lake, ski areas on King Ridge, and Interstate 89 edging through the lush woodlands.

Soon, you arrive at an ample parking space at the end of the road with still another wide-open view to the south. In the distance Grand Monadnock, Crotched Mountain, the Uncanoonuc Mountains, hilltops of Massachusetts, and (on clear days) the Boston skyline are visible. Nearby you can see the Mink Hills and Merrimack River.

The summit trail begins opposite the parking lot overview and to the right as you face the granite top of Mount Kearsarge. The footpath is well cut, wide, and rises at an easy angle upward through clusters of golden, cherry, and paper birch.

In short order, an overlook of the auto road to the south appears and gives you a sense of more high views to come farther up the summit.

Around this area is a good place to spot shelf ferns (look for triangular fronds) and interrupted ferns, which have spore-bearing leaflets located midway on ("interrupting") their three-to-four stalks.

Hewn logs set here and there across the trail help prevent erosion and also make the walk easier. As always, watch your step over the flat granite surface and smooth, barkless, slippery logs during the wet season.

Several drainage channels have been constructed crossing the trail to capture spring runoff of winter snow and ice. Although it can be invigorating for the spirit to be outdoors in spring, it's also a time to anticipate water flow from rain, mud, and black-fly seasons. Water bars across the pathway help divert water, which, if left to puddle, can erode the trail and turn into breeding sites for insects.

Granite ledges to the side of the trail winding its gentle way back and forth offer spectacular views of the long rolling hills below. Shortly after you pass one of the early lookouts (about 0.4 mile), a small spring outflow crosses the trail from a small pool of spring water.

As you proceed, keep watch for low bush blueberries cropping out of cracks in the rocks. Chipmunks in this section were plentiful, darting in and out of the ferns when we were there.

The trail then takes you through a mix of hemlock and spruce, which can be distinguished from each other in many ways. While hemlock grow in broad, flat-topped silhouettes, spruce are shaped more in a pyramidal point. Hemlock needles are short, flat, arranged in two rows on the twig, and silver-lined beneath. They're smooth to the touch. Four-sided spruce needles, on the other hand, prickle to the touch and feel more resistant. They grow in dense spirals around the twigs.

After passing another spring a short distance ahead as the trail leads into more scattered woods, the fire and radio towers come into view. The trail levels again, winding along flat granite slabs.

At this point the trail clearly coincides with an old carriage road used to convey sightseers to a point where the bald summit takes a decidedly upward angle, impassable for carriage travel. The road was built in 1873 by the Warner & Kearsarge Road Company as part of a toll road from Warner Village to the summit. Over thirty years the road deteriorated, but repairs to the road continued for another three decades. In 1918, the Society for the Protection of New Hampshire Forests bought land on the mountain and named the 521-acre reservation Rollins Memorial Park in honor of Governor Frank W. Rollins, a founder of the society. The society transferred

*The Mount
Kearsarge fire
tower.*

the land to the state, which established a state park here
in 1950.

After another fifty feet or so, the trail moves more into
the open. Tree growth becomes shorter; juniper bushes
appear. Then white trail blazes on the bare granite surface
lead the way above treeline toward the summit.

This peak is windy most of the time; it's advisable to
wear a windbreaker. One day we climbed this trail, the
wind-velocity readings at the fire tower recorded gusts
of 20 MPH.

The fire lookout ranger is accustomed to guests. If you're curious about the tower and what you can see from the top, climb the forty steps and enjoy the extraordinary view out of the wind.

As you approach the fire tower, you'll notice a footpath sign pointing in the direction of Winslow State Park. The Winslow Trail on the north side of the mountain descends one mile and is blazed with red dots.

As the counterpart to Rollins State Park, Winslow State Park Trail in Wilmot on the north side of Mount Kearsarge leaves from a large picnic area that once was a nineteenth-century hotel called the Winslow House. Granite blocks of a cellar hole are all that remain.

Other Mountains Seen from the Mount Kearsarge Summit

Mountain	Miles
Belknap	26.2
Pawtuckaway	37.0
Uncanoonuc	30.8
Cramer Hill	16.6
Grand Monadnock	38.2
Sunapee	11.0
Croydon Peak	19.4
Killington, Vt.	51.6
Cardigan	18.6
Cannon	54.0
Washington	67.2

The rocky, wide-open summit of Mount Kearsarge is irresistible for lounging and looking. In a short while, huge dragonflies will likely whiz through the air and hover around mountain walkers sprawled on the granite peak, reluctant to descend.

Getting There

Heading either south or north on I-89, turn off at Exit 9 onto Route 103. Drive into the center of Warner on the east side of the interstate and turn onto Kearsarge Mountain Road, veering immediately to the left at a Y junction. Follow Kearsarge Mountain Road to the Rollins State Park sign and turn right. Drive 5 miles to the park entrance.

Other Information

Rollins State Park
Warner, NH 03278
603-456-3808
Opens the first week in May; closes November 7.

Mount Kearsarge Indian Museum

Medicine Woods Path (Loop)

Warner

- **0.25 mile**
- **20 minutes**
- **easy**

An identification trail of plants, shrubs, and trees used by Native Americans for food, medicine, and dyes.

This makes a wonderful family outing. The well-designed museum honors and celebrates the Native American culture with an extraordinary collection of artifacts and a nature trail showing many of the plants used for medicines by Native Americans.

Visitors are reminded of the peace and quiet of the forest as they read an inscription by Chief Luther Standing Bear at the entrance to Medicine Woods: *When we enter the forest, we must do so quietly and unobtrusively, for only when we enter on nature's terms will the forest reveal to us her greatest secrets, her hidden treasures.* Thoughtful sayings such as this exercise the mind and spirit on this short, fascinating identification trail of Native American plants, shrubs, and trees.

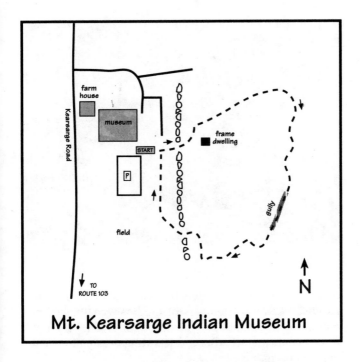

Mt. Kearsarge Indian Museum

Trained guides lead tours, if you'd like, around the two-acre woodland enclosure, but the path is clearly defined with stones. Turnoffs keep visitors from trampling the delicate wildflowers.

At the entrance, children probably will want to try the tree-stump seats or peek into an Abenaki dome-shaped frame covered with birch bark. Both of these areas are reserved for storytelling.

The short path loops to the left past indigenous species used by Native Americans for medicines, dyes,

This Abenaki frame will be covered with bark.

and food. Museum founders Bud and Nancy Thompson, as well as Native members of the board, actively contribute to the plantings, and throughout the year outdoor events are scheduled celebrating seasonal growth and thanksgiving.

The day we were there, little colored bows had been tied to an evergreen in memory of Sachem Silverstar. In a way, the seed idea for the museum was planted when Bud Thompson was seven years old and the strapping Pequot chief walked into his classroom, leaving a lasting impression on the second grader.

As Bud grew older and more inspired by the Indian legacy, he increased his collection of Indian artifacts over the years until he ended up with an eye-dazzling array of finely crafted baskets, snowshoes, pottery, and many other objects of beauty from twenty-five Indian nations. Never deviating from his long-term goal, Bud and his wife, Nancy, settled in Warner and built the museum and medicine trail, dedicating the collection in 1992. His lifework was to come full circle when Chief Silverstar's son planned to attend the ceremony, but the son died a month before the opening. However, three years later, Silverstar's granddaughter appeared to plant and dedicate a tree.

On the interpretive path, an informative sign at the base of each plant gives the common and Latin name and how individual plants were used by various tribes. Some of the species along the first part of the path include jack-in-the-pulpit, once used as a cough remedy; blood root used as a dye; partridgeberry, whose red berries winter over for spring foraging; and arrowwood (a viburnum), crafted into arrow shafts. The white ash tree seemed particularly useful: the Penobscot used the leaves of the white ash for a decoction to give women after childbirth. The Mohawk used drops of liquid from heated white ash logs for earache. And the wood of the ash was a favorite for making baskets and fish spears, and was used in canoe and snowshoe manufacture.

The path descends a slight incline into a shallow valley. Cross a footbridge over a moist culvert. A magnificent view of the meadow and mountain opens up at the edge of the forest beyond the stone wall. The Ojibway prayer on a plaque near this sight seems a fitting one: *Grandfather, Sacred One, Teach us love, compassion and honor that we may heal the earth and heal each other.*

Pass through the entrance in the stone wall, and stroll up a wide swath of grass paralleling a pasture. On

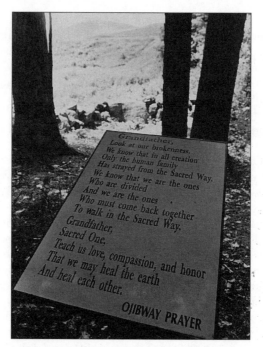

An Ojibway prayer in Medicine Woods.

the right in the stone wall ingenious dirt wells have been built on top of the wall. These natural field-stone containers place a series of plants at eye level for smaller children.

Strangely enough, the prickly-pear cactus, found primarily in the Southwest, survives the inhospitable winter here and resurrects in the wall each spring. Don't touch. (The pear-shaped edible fruits are collected with gloves because of irritating prickles.) The yucca, a south-western traveler now growing in most states, sends up its tall stalk of white bell flowers; the spiny leaves of this "silkgrass" furnish fibrous threads for weaving.

Along the pasture fence is a linden tree (also called basswood) with heart-shaped leaves; Native Americans wove its inner bark into rope. In this bright sunny area, sun chokes (also called Jerusalem artichokes) average three to four feet tall with golden sunflowers. In fall their edible spudlike tubers are dug up and eaten. Sometimes they can be found in local supermarkets.

A large teepee crowns the hill behind the museum on the pasture side of the fence. Several celebrations and educational programs are held throughout the year in field and forest.

Reenter the stone wall to your right. A bench has been set conveniently beneath the shade of the trees for reflection: *Behold, my brothers, the spring has come,* announces Chief Sitting Bull. *It is through this mysterious power that we too have our being. And we therefore yield to our neighbors (even our animal neighbors) the same right as ourselves to inhabit this land.*

Much of the plant knowledge shared by the People of the Dawn (Abenaki) and other Native Americans centuries ago still applies today. Fragrant bayberry scents our soaps and candles. Pipsissewas and wintergreen ease our aching muscles. Bergamot and other wildflowers are brewed as herbal teas. Recently, ancient species of teosinte and other Indian corn have been grown experimentally in the Warner area. The Indian Museum and Medicine Woods actively engage visitors in an awareness of the land and a respect for use without abuse.

Getting There

From Exit 8 off I-89 take NH 103 west for 1.3 miles through the town of Warner, following signs to the Indian Museum. Turn right onto Kearsarge Mountain Road and drive 1.1 miles. The museum is clearly marked on the right. Park beside the barnlike building. The Medicine Woods Path is opposite the museum entrance.

Other Information

The museum (603-456-2600) is open May through October, Monday through Saturday 10:00 A.M. to 5:00 P.M., Sunday 12:00 NOON to 6:00 P.M. Tours of the museum leave on the hour. The "Dreamcatcher" museum starts with a section devoted to objects found in the region, dating back to the Woodland Peoples. Other noteworthy artifacts include an eighteen-foot canoe, Cree bittenwork (teeth designs in bark), basketry by Tomah Joseph, delicate beadwork, and a towering Indian statue carved from a mammoth tree trunk.

Gile State Forest

Gardner Memorial Wayside Park

Springfield

Old Mill Site Trail

- **0.22 mile**
- **15 minutes**
- **easy**

---

*A short and sweet brookside walk to boulder-wall
remnants of a nineteenth-century mill.*

Begin the first of these two enjoyable trails at the Gardner Memorial Wayside Park, a small off-highway oasis
maintained by the New Hampshire Parks Department.

To reach the Old Mill Site, follow wide, shallow
Kimpton Brook from a footbridge at the far end of the
parking area. A picnic table stands alone here in an inviting location beside the stream, a charming spot to lunch,
snack, or rest.

The trailhead for this pleasant meander is easily
found on the far side of the footbridge.

A sign directs the way to both the Old Mill Site and
Butterfield Pond Trails. The pathway to the Old Mill Site
starts at the right immediately after the bridge.

The first walk takes you through mixed airy woods
of fir and hemlock and alongside the crystalline brook

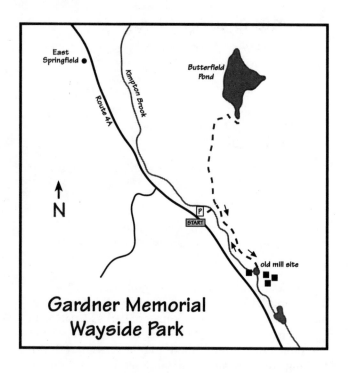

Gardner Memorial
Wayside Park

on the right for the entire distance. Gentle plashing of the
stream accompanies you as you ease down the needle-
strewn trail.

For such a short stroll, this trail offers an unusual
diversity of conspicuous plant life. The common bracken
fern is plentiful; you can recognize it by its three flat, triangular blades horizontal to the ground. They grow
about two feet high on a thin stem.

Many three-leaf, three-petaled trillium grow here, too, noticeable especially in spring for their carmine-colored trio of petals offset by a trio of graceful elongated leaves. This burgundy variety is known as "wake-robin." The goldthread ground cover also has triple leaves, and gold-colored roots. Bluebead lilies with their own three broad, sturdy, shiny leaves are evident, particularly toward fall when navy beads dot the end of a long, thin straight stem.

Continue among the fir and hemlock. The evergreens provide a needle carpet among the exposed roots; watch your step.

About 500 feet from the trailhead, the right side of the trail opens onto the brook and a dam built from mammoth chunks of granite comes into view.

This end point makes a good spot to sit and enjoy the everlasting play between water and stone.

Return to the trail and follow it straight sixty more feet to a Y junction. Take the right path (the left one soon peters out) for a closer view of the dam. Hefty stones remain piled above the granite base along the brook where the river was channeled for the mill. Only the foundation of the mill remains.

Return to the trailhead as you came.

Getting There

From I-89 take Exit 12A north to Springfield. From the Springfield post office drive 0.1 mile to the bottom of the hill. At the sign to NH 4A, turn right onto Four Corners Road and drive past the Springfield Meeting House on the left. At 0.8 mile veer left (do not take Bowman Road). At 1.9 miles turn right onto NH 4A south (right). You are now driving through Gile State Forest. Drive 3.3 miles on NH 4A south to a sign on the left for Gardner Memorial Wayside Park, on the left.

Affiliated Organizations

New Hampshire Parks and Recreation
P.O. Box 856
Concord, NH 03302
603-271-3254

Gile State Forest
Butterfield Pond Trail
Springfield

- **0.87 mile**
- **45 minutes**
- **moderate**

A deep woods walk to an isolated, quiet, primeval-like pond encircled with woods.

The pathway to Butterfield Pond begins on the forest side of the footbridge. Walk straight ahead from the bridge and ascend a gentle, sometimes wet, earthen trail that can be rocky and rooty in the first 100 feet.

The ascent is easy through mixed woods. In 300 feet turn right as the sign directs and continue a mild steady ascent on a narrower trail. Tree roots are ample enough to require careful watching to avoid tripping or slipping. In spring bluebead lilies grow alongside the trail beneath the beech, hemlock, and fir and unfurl their light yellow six-petal flowers. In fall shiny, deep blue bead-like berries (inedible) replace the flowers.

The trail is blazed with rectangular metal yellow markers on the trees. The growth of the rich green club moss at trailside contrasts with the embedded white quartzite patches exposed along the way.

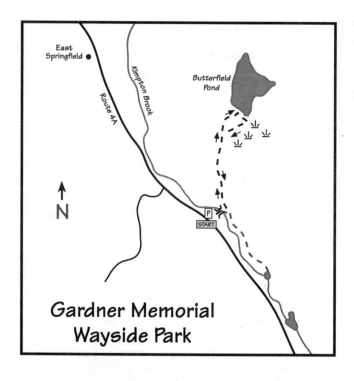

East
Springfield ●

Route 4A

Kimpton Brook

Butterfield
Pond

P
START

↑
N

Gardner Memorial
Wayside Park

At 0.2 mile a beech forest appears and with it spacious eye-level views (because of the tall gray branchless trunks). This section has a kind of abstract quality to it. In fact, a uniform subforest such as this shows off these dominant trees—as if the beeches long ago had won the battle and usurped the territory for themselves, using the shade they cast as their major weapon.

A short distance ahead, pass through an opening in a stone wall and enter a ramshackle boulder area with huge shapes and shadows. Transitions of one short scene to another add a visual flourish to a walk in this special undeveloped tract of New Hampshire.

Along the way note the occasional giant girth of white birches and beeches that stand out all the more compared to the sapling growth of the other trees.

Approach a tannin-dark swamp on the right by descending a slight incline at 0.36 mile. The trail skirts the small grassy swamp, crosses a thick rotting log, and continues a few feet through grassy, branchy overgrowth. The pathway is solid underfoot. Nevertheless, a good way to walk through overgrowth such as this is to hold your arms upright in front of your head (your hands facing each other and level to the top of your head). This way your forearms hit the shrubbery and branches before the overgrowth hits your face. You have to pass through less than twenty feet of the brush.

At 0.4 mile the pond comes into view on the left, but continue straight ahead on the trail, crossing the yard-wide outlet of the pond into the swamp. This juncture between pond and swamp gives a striking picture of the stark difference between the brackish cul-de-sac of the swamp on the right and the deep blue expanse of the fresh pond on the left.

Take a few steps over a small rise in the trail and walk down to the left to the shore of the pond at 0.42 mile.

The secluded quiet here is disturbed at most by croaking frogs and bickering blue jays. Tree-lined and silent, Butterfield Pond sprouts a few white and yellow waterlilies along the shore, luring you for a sit-down and a stare.

Life in and around ponds is plentiful and fascinating. One of the most common examples of pond life is frogs, born in the water as tadpoles and surfacing as adults. Neckless and with powerful hind legs that propel them two to three feet or more, frogs are generally thin and smooth compared to toads, which are squat and warty. Their eyes are adapted especially to noticing such moving objects as insects, worms, and spiders. When they detect such a dinner-in-motion, frogs dart their

The silence and untamed beauty of Butterfield Pond is well worth a little bushwhacking.

long, sticky tongues (which are connected to the *front* of their mouths) forward at great speed to catch the unlucky prey. Here the most likely frog you'll spot is the leopard frog, a dark green-brown species with yellow and white bars, found in nearly every pond. If you're inclined to grasp a leopard frog, you can "hypnotize" the slippery creature by placing it on its back and stroking its belly; let loose and the relaxed frog will remain in place for a few minutes.

Return to the trailhead by the same path.

Getting There

From I-89 take Exit 12A north to Springfield. From the Springfield post office drive 0.1 mile to the bottom of the hill. At the sign to NH 4A, turn right onto Four Corners Road and drive past the Springfield Meeting House on the left. At 0.8 mile veer left (do not take Bowman Road). At 1.9 miles turn right onto NH 4A south (right). You are now driving through Gile State Forest. Drive 3.3 miles on NH 4A south to a sign on the left for Gardner Memorial Wayside Park on the left.

Affiliated Organizations

New Hampshire Parks and Recreation
P.O. Box 856
Concord, NH 03302
603-271-3254

Philbrick-Cricenti Bog

Peek Hole, Tundra Garden, Quaking, & Bog Peril Identification Trails (Loops)

New London

- **0.75 mile**
- **1 hour and 20 minutes**
- **easy**

A self-guided boardwalk tour over a thick mat of unique arctic tundra plants growing atop a deep glacial pond.

The wetlands known as peatlands are divided into two types: fens, which have a land source of running water to replenish their oxygen content; and bogs, which are rejuvenated only by rainfall. Certain indicator plants are found in both fens and bogs—tamaracks, pitcher plants, cranberries, swamp loosestrife. All of these are found at Philbrick-Cricenti Bog.

Originally, this fascinating site was a gravel-bed pool born of a glacier melting 10,000 years ago at the end of the last Ice Age. Gradually, arctic plants of leatherleaf, sedge, bog rosemary, and cotton grass along the shoreline grew toward the center of the pool, slowly tangling and thickening. Except for some identified off-limits sections,

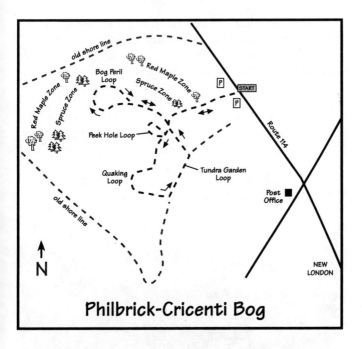

Philbrick-Cricenti Bog

this "quaking mat" is spongy but perfectly safe to walk along on the boardwalks laid out for these trails.

This singular twenty-five-acre site is a glowing example of how cooperation and financial support combine to benefit the public. It has been saved through joint efforts by the U.S. Heritage Preservation and Recreation Commission; New Hampshire Department of Economic Resources and Development; the New London Conservation Commission; and private support from the Philbrick, Cricenti, and Cleveland families.

Pick up a flier from a pocket on the covered sign-board at the trailhead. The map indicates twenty-one stops on three interconnected loop trails. Miniature drawings will help walkers to identify the bog cranberry, bog rosemary, cotton grass, sedge, and other flora. A colored picture of the "flower of the week" also is posted. When we visited the bog during the first week of July, the flower was calopogon, a yellow-crested wild pink orchid, which indeed could be seen growing above the quaking bog mat.

A short gravel access path runs on top of the roots of decayed royal ferns. Now taller cinnamon ferns (often

Visitors at Cricenti Bog stay on boardwalks floating on a twenty-five-foot deep mat of vegetation.

growing in circular clusters) and five-foot-high ostrich ferns (which taper at top and bottom like a feathered plume) grow here. In 100 feet you come to a larger map on a central signboard at a junction. Despite the many little loops and diversions, it's difficult to get "bogged" down because all paths eventually return to this point.

Turn left and after twenty feet, turn right at a juncture marked Peekhole Loop. Immediately, there's a noticeable change in the bogscape. The red maple give way to spindly black spruce and tamarack that thrive on acidic peat vegetation. Black spruce propagates new trees by putting down new roots. This asexual activity known as "layering" works quite efficiently on the edge of the Philbrick-Cricenti Bog.

Near the spruce you'll see the lacy blue-green of the tamarack, or American larch. The short needles of this conifer grow in tufts of a dozen or so straight from the twigs themselves, and its cones are short and fat. Unlike most conifers, the tamarack sheds its needles in the fall, giving the trees a dead appearance until spring. The scruffy bark and twisted branches of tamarack seem rather menacing, but run a hand along the new needles of a sapling and you'll find them silky soft.

At the edge of the mat of sphagnum moss (also called peat) are the heath plants, including sheep laurel and highbush blueberries. In about 500 feet you come to an extensive boardwalk on the open bog. Sticking up from one of several watery depressions is a pole that looks like a long-handled spoon in a cauldron of dark broth. The pole is there for visitors to pull out to see for themselves how deep the bog is. The word "bog" derives from the Celtic *Bocc,* meaning soft. Take one step off the boardwalk and you could be, as the saying goes, in way over your head.

Stops 10–13 are on the open Tundra Garden Loop. Here you will see several carnivorous pitcher plants. The low-lying green or purple pitcher plants are noticeable for their deep cuplike flowers with folded-in petals. The trap, half-filled with water, is ingeniously designed to drown hapless insects struggling to escape. The plants secrete enzymes that allow them to absorb

Pitcher plants collect rainwater and unsuspecting insects, which they digest with specially secreted enzymes.

insects, providing the pitcher plants with nitrogen. Bog rosemary (which looks similar to kitchen rosemary) proliferates in the red-colored sphagnum moss carpet. The fibrous root system of the sedge and this sphagnum moss decay and settle at the bottom and add bulk to the mat.

At 0.2 mile you segue onto the Quaking Loop. Here the bog mat is extremely thin, and the slightest weighty provocation causes the boardwalk to jiggle and shake. (But fear not, it's all quite safe if you use caution.)

Enter the birch, maple, and evergreen forest where more typical woodland plants such as the bluebead lily grow. Turn left, leaving the boardwalk for a pine-needle and root-strewn path. Watch your step in the tangle of roots that cling to the sparse topsoil as you wend your way back to the starting point of the first loop.

At 0.37 mile you come once again to the central signboard. This time turn right for the last (and scariest) Peril Loop. When you come to the loop junction fifty feet ahead, turn left. Along here you can distinguish thin, large chartreuse areas that don't look like the darker, thicker, and stronger vegetation. Those telltale patches are where moose, deer, a cow, or a horse wandered into the bog and were swallowed by it. Quaking tundra is just as dangerous as quicksand for unknowing interlopers. This is one reason visitors are asked to leave their dogs home.

At 0.5 mile re-enter the dwarfed spruce and tamarack on the edge of the bog and finish the Peril Loop at 0.6 mile. It's only a short walk back to the central signboard. Turn left at 0.7 mile, and return on the gravel access path to the parking area.

A few years ago the Philbrick-Cricenti Bog received the Homer Lucas Landscape Award from the New England Wild Flower Society because the area was judged to be "an outstanding public garden displaying native plants. The bog offers visitors a beautiful and tranquil retreat as well as a fascinating opportunity to learn about a distinctive natural habitat." We heartily concur.

Getting There

From the U.S. Post Office and Cricenti's Market in New London, turn left onto Newport Road. Drive 0.25 mile, passing large roadside boulders on the right. Opposite these on the left are the trailhead and sign partially hidden in the trees. A wide shoulder on the left allows for parking.

Other Information

Closed 6:00 P.M. to 6:00 A.M. Children under fourteen must be with responsible adults.

Note: Fliers and maps for other footpaths in the area are available at the town clerk's office, library, and bookstores.

Mount Sunapee State Park
Lake Solitude Trail
Newbury

- **2 miles**
- **1 hour and 30 minutes**
- **moderate**

*A gentle wooded descent along the southeastern
slope of Mount Sunapee to White Ledges and
panoramic views of a pristine glacial lake and the
Monadnock-Sunapee Greenway beyond.*

A spectacular outing awaits you here. The views are
breathtaking, the wood scenes to Lake Solitude varied
and pleasing, the destination named exactly right.

If you're feeling very energetic, you can climb to the
summit of Mount Sunapee by following the broad,
cleared section beneath the chairlift, although this doubles the walking length. If you'd rather not climb the
mountain, ride the chairlift to the top for easier access to
the Lake Solitude trailhead. The ride does give you
another enjoyable dimension to this walk.

At the main lodge (opens Memorial Day) purchase
round-trip chairlift tickets. The ride to the 2,743-foot summit takes twenty minutes and is a delightful treat. On a
clear blue day you're literally sitting on top of the world.

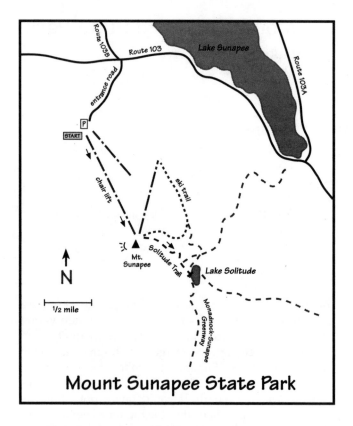

Mount Sunapee State Park

With the summit lodge/concession behind you, follow the prominent sign To All Trails on the right. A double white blaze and orange arrow on a cement block mark the trailhead. Three trail signs with arrows point to various pathways. The Lake Solitude sign indicates a descent down a wide ski slope. To the left as the ski run winds over the eastern slope is a wide-open view of nine-mile-long Lake Sunapee. The name of the lake comes from the Penacook Indian language and means "wild goose water." During the nineteenth century steamboats with summering tourists plied the lake waters, and today Sunapee remains a major recreational area.

If you cross this grassy area in spring you'll see patches of spring beauties dotting the slope. Their pink-and-white five-petal blooms hug the alpine soil.

Heading straight toward the woods, at 0.4 mile is a sign: Solitude Trail and Lake Solitude. Follow the narrow footpath with orange blazes into the fir and spruce forest.

Spring at these high altitudes comes much later and often lasts through June. At this time of year these woods are truly enchanting. A grove of white birch and the shrub hobblebush (known also as bridal wreath for its lacy white spring flower clusters) decorates the open ravine.

This half of the walk meanders up and down over rocks and roots, so watch your step. Nestled in the moss and clumps of grass are painted trillium (with three leaves and three white petals with red bases) and wake-robin (a burgundy-colored trillium). The high-altitude bluebead lily proliferates on the trailside. First in the spring come the three bluish-green oval leaves, then the pale yellow drooping flowers, and then toward fall its purple-blue berries.

At 0.7 mile the path pitches upward and to the left through beech, birch, and spruce forest. On a rise you come to a small whaleback of granite, an elongated, humplike protrusion left over from glacial movements

A trio of painted trillium.

that eroded away softer earth. To your left an orange arrow painted on this rounded glacial drift points to Lake Solitude (a 0.6-mile descent). But the White Ledges straight ahead are your final destination.

Proceed up and over the whaleback; a magical scene awaits you. Far below nestled in a sea of green is the dark gleaming glacial lake. Lake Solitude fits its name most during the week. This spot, with swallows and raptors soaring high over the tannin-darkened lake water, is one of isolated splendor. Your serenity won't be too ruffled by the whoops of excited children crying, "It's awesome!" These ledges mark the terminus of the forty-nine-mile Monadnock-Sunapee Greenway, a long green corridor and trail stretching to the south. Conceived by AMC President Allen Chamberlain in 1919 and built in 1921 by the Society for the Protection of New Hampshire Forests, this unique river of trees and trail follows open ridgelines and wooded valleys from Grand Monadnock north to Mount Sunapee. The pathway continues to be protected by private landowners and conservation groups.

Return by the same trail, saving your reserves for the last 0.3 mile back up the steep ski slope. You'll have time to get your breath back on the chairlift ride back down—if it isn't taken away again by the views of Lake Sunapee and the White Mountains to the north.

Getting There

From I-89 take Exit 9 and drive west on NH 103 to the town of Newbury (approximately 16 miles). From the pergola and boat launch on the lake, drive 3 more miles on NH 103. Turn left at the large Mount Sunapee State Park access road (Mount Sunapee Acres Road) that leads to the parking lot.

Other Information

Some other hiking trails in the park include the Newbury Trail, Rim Trail, Eagles Nest, and Porky's Ski Trail. Telephone: 603-763-2356.

John Hay National Wildlife Refuge (The Fells)

Forest Ecology Identification Trail

Newbury

- **1 mile**
- **1 hour (plus 30-minute walk round trip to estate)**
- **moderate**

Twenty-seven marked ecological observations encompass the Lake Sunapee shore, woods, and brook at this National Wildlife Refuge.

Besides being the most prominent summer resident on Lake Sunapee later in his life, John Milton Hay (1838–1905) was an influential statesman and diplomat for much of his life. Among other accomplishments, Hay was assistant private secretary to President Lincoln and secretary of state under Presidents William McKinley and Theodore Roosevelt. A naturalist and writer, Hay took keen interest in developing the woodland and lakeshore settings of his summer home, the Fells.

In 1891 Hay transformed stretches of pasture on a ridge (fells) into a formal rock garden, rose terrace, and walled Pan garden with stone walls, Oriental plants, and statuary. Today the summer house serves as a conserva-

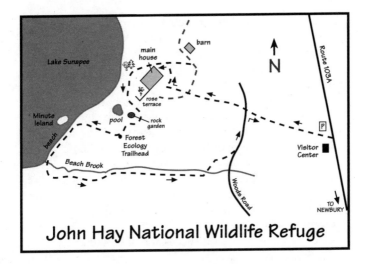

John Hay National Wildlife Refuge

tion center and the focus for educational programs. Some recent events include a garden party/art show, a tour of nurseries in Vermont, and a fern workshop.

Getting to the main house and trailhead is half the fun on this multifaceted walk. The entrance road is lined with stately oak, 200-year-old sugar maple, and a variety of wildflowers. As you near the great house, billows of rhododendrons adorn the pebble drive and lawn. The optimal time to catch them in radiant splendor is the second half of June.

Pass to the right of the courtyard, which actually faces the back of the house, and walk along the front piazza area. Inside you may pick up a brochure, talk to the ranger, and tour the house.

Continue walking past the front of the house, through the rose terrace to the south, and down to the rock garden pool. This attractive outcrop of granite with meandering pathways and 400 plant species was designed in the 1930s by John Hay's son, archaeologist Clarence Hay, and his wife, Alice, who added more than 100 acres to the estate.

Look down the southwest slope toward Lake Sunapee. About midway down is a brown sign pointing to the Forest Ecology Trail. Head toward the lake and duck into the shade of the pasture pines to the right.

This trail has stops with educational descriptions of the local ecosystem. Forest Succession is the first stop (of twenty-seven) and describes how open fields are reclaimed by trees to make a forest. Abandoned pastures succumb to shrubs. Pines like these follow shrubs, then are crowded in turn by a succession of taller hardwoods.

Birch, red spruce, and Norway pines (stop 2) then take over as transitional species. The Norway or red pines have tall straight trunks often used for telephone and electrical poles.

Just beyond the white birches is a double blaze. Continue straight to the next blaze. The trail sign points to the left. Descend past erratic boulders deposited here by glacial ice sheets (stop 4) and through a shady hemlock forest to an area of second-growth red maple and sprouting stumps. These are monotypic growth or one species of one age (stop 9).

Lake Sunapee (stop 10) is a good spot for lunch or a snack. Cut off from the shore by a narrow channel of water is Minute Island, which has a prominent large boulder (another glacial erratic) on it. Boaters anchor in the shoals of the idyllic little island. Unfortunately, the roar of their motors is as disturbing as noise from a high-

The wildflowers at the Fells attract this tiger swallowtail butterfly.

way, but it was probably a lot worse in the good old days: in 1905 you could purchase a $2 train ticket in Boston, take a steamboat lunch cruise, and be home by supper. Steamers with puffing smokestacks and loud whistles vied for tourists.

Nevertheless, due to visionaries like summer residents Hay in Newbury and Saint-Gaudens in Cornish, large tracts of farmland were preserved. In fact, mill owner Albert E. Pillsbury (for whom Pillsbury State Park is named) became one of nine founders of the Society for the Protection of New Hampshire Forests, to which Clarence and Alice Hay deeded most of the Fells estate of 675 acres in 1960. In 1972 the remainder of the estate was deeded to the U.S. Fish and Wildlife Service.

This small rock-and-tree island appears where the trail meets the shoreline of nine-mile-long Lake Sunapee.

Lake Sunapee is three miles wide and nine miles long. It is smaller than Lake Winnipesaukee, but at 1,000 feet in elevation, it does enjoy the distinction of being twice as high.

The common shadbush and less common tupelo (stop 13) grow on the shoreline at about 0.4 mile. The shadbush blooms around the same time of spring when shad and salmon used to run up these northern streams to spawn. It grows tree-size in New Hampshire; most people know it by another name, serviceberry. Plum-shaped alternate leaves, white long-petaled blossoms in early spring, and burgundy-colored berries distinguish it.

Tupelo, or black gum, trees have stiff horizontal twigs, smooth shiny oval-shaped leaves, and the dark blue fruit characteristic of many dogwoods. The fruits of both are eaten by birds and mammals.

At 0.7 mile the trail comes out on a small sandy beach with views of the southern end of the lake and 2,700-foot Mount Sunapee. Behind the beach and to the left (facing the lake) is the next blaze. Although the trail brochure indicates a shortcut back to the house, it was grown in when we were there. We advise sticking to the main trail.

Cross Beech Brook and gradually ascend the riverbank, bypassing serene pools, plashing rivulets, and mossy granite steps (stop 25). When you reach the Woods Road, turn left and walk another 0.1 mile back to the junction of Woods Road with the main entrance road.

Return on the entrance road to the parking lot.

Getting There

From NH 103 in Newbury, turn onto NH 103A and drive 2.2 miles to the Hay Estate sign on the left. Park at the gatehouse parking lot immediately next to NH 103A. Visitors are requested to walk the 0.3-mile hard-packed entrance road to the main house and gardens.

Other Information

The Hay Estate
P.O. Box 276
Newbury, NH 03255
603-763-4789 or 2452

Open 10:00 A.M. to 6:00 P.M. weekends and holidays from late May to Columbus Day. A nominal fee soon to be established.

Stoney Brook Audubon Wildlife Sanctuary

Marsh View Trail (Loop)

Newbury

- **1 mile**
- **1 hour and 15 minutes**
- **easy**
- **boots recommended**

Pleasant and interesting for the entire family, this well-designed, flat trail passes through young evergreen woods before skirting an engrossing marsh.

Swamps, bogs, and marshes are all wetlands, but the differences among them can be confusing. A swamp is generally defined as a spongy land saturated but not necessarily covered with water. A bog is usually considered an acidic wetland of decaying moss and peat with little circulation of water. A marsh is a wetland with sparse trees but lots of tussock sedge, pickerelweed, and cattails. This walk takes you to a marsh through healthy stands of hemlock and pine.

Park in the small area at the trailhead directly off Chalk Pond Road. Marsh View Trail is one of two trails (and, we think, the better one) in the Stoney Brook Wildlife Sanctuary. (The longer Beech Hill Trail is

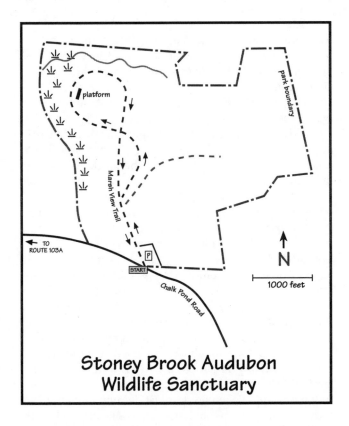

Stoney Brook Audubon Wildlife Sanctuary

located three-quarters of a mile farther ahead on Chalk Pond Road.)

The Marsh View Trail begins on the old logging road to the left of the trailhead parking area. A mailbox with brochures inside marks the start of the trail, which is blazed with red metal rectangles nailed to tree trunks.

After a few gentle rises on the grassy tote road, the trail remains graded and flat nearly the entire walk.

The woods at the outset are relatively thin and young; they're fast, new growth appearing after extensive logging in years past. This is wetland, so in some spots expect the trail/road's old wheel ruts to be full of water; they're easily bypassed.

Old stone walls line the trail sporadically before disappearing altogether. In about a quarter of a mile at a Y junction with a noticeably large hemlock, veer right onto the footpath and a slight incline. This junction begins a figure-eight loop. The trail is intelligently laid out so that very little scenery is repeated on your walk.

The pathway now passes through thicker but still mostly young woodland dominated by hemlock and fir. The latter, especially the fragrant balsam fir, are soft feeling, their short, blunt needles marked with white lines underneath. This section of the trail is a good place to stop and compare the soft, "friendly" fir needles with the "sharp" spruce (four-sided, tight around the branch) and hemlock (short, flat on two flattened rows).

But look down, too. In this area of discontinued logging, with many fallen trunks deteriorating and wetlands nearby, plenty of British soldiers are afoot. These tiny pinheaded lichen favor moist decaying materials to grow their gray green half-inch stalks topped with bright red caps.

Spruce and fir grow thicker as the trail curves left and, about 0.3 mile into the walk, crosses the tote road that began the trail. Proceed directly across the road and into the trees again, still following the red-blazed trail. This section weaves in and out of the evergreens, which

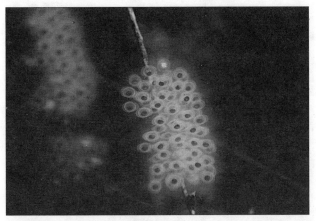

Salamanders, efts, newts, and other amphibians lay their eggs in trailside ditches and canals.

carpet the earth with needles, dampening the already quiet woods. More fallen logs are noticeable here.

About 100 feet after crossing the road, the marsh appears on the left.

Another 0.1 mile and a pleasant surprise suddenly appears—a well-built observation deck. The platform is situated immediately to the right of the trail on slightly higher ground overlooking the marsh. Only a dozen steps up, the deck makes an ideal spot to rest, savor the silence, do some bird-watching, and listen to the medley of birdcalls. We watched a sky drama of three agitated, cawing crows divebomb and speed-chase a hawk away. Good place here for a snack and drink, too. You can see the sedge type of growth that defines a marsh. Dead

Tamarack is easily identified by the clusters of soft needles on both sides of its branches.

trunks stick out of the high grassy expanse, signifying that the constant water has killed a few trees.

Continue on the trail left of the platform and re-enter the pine and fir. In about 100 feet, the path narrows to the edge of a smaller young marsh in development. Turn right along the spongy edge for another 100 feet to the tote road that started the walk; it's plainly visible and marks about a half-mile into the walk.

Return down the road toward the trailhead parking area, passing where the trail crossed the road, making the first part of the figure-eight loop.

About another 100 feet beyond this trail crossing, the trail/road descends into a watery spillover from the marsh. Take your time through here, not so much to keep your boots dry but to see the abundant smaller life forms.

The spillover here is part of an interesting survival strategy. In spring salamanders and other amphibians deposit eggs in clusters on grass stalks submerged in the small watery pools of road ruts and ditches. In these transient vernal pools of snowmelt and rain the eggs can mature undisturbed by fish and other predators. By the time the pools dry up the eggs have hatched and the new amphibians have gone their way.

Make your way across two fallen logs over a watery section and continue down the tote road trail, soon passing the Y junction with the outsized hemlock where you started the figure-eight. The last leg to the trailhead is easy going and a pleasant ending.

Getting There

In Newbury on Route 103 at the southeastern end of Lake Sunapee, take Route 103A north for 2.9 miles. Turn right onto Chalk Pond Road and drive 1.3 miles. Opposite a residence, a small Audubon sign on the left of the road marks the entrance. Park immediately to the right in the trailhead parking area.

Other Information

Audubon Society of New Hampshire
3 Silk Farm Road
Concord, NH 03301
603-224-9909

Meriden Bird Club Sanctuary

Meriden Bird Club Sanctuary Trail (Loop)

Meriden

- **1.4 miles**
- **1 hour**
- **moderate**

A woodland walk through the first bird sanctuary in America, featuring an ornate commemorative birdbath and natural bark birdhouses.

At the turn of the twentieth century when widespread fashion included wearing hats with bird feathers, Ernest Harold Baynes (1868–1925) had a different idea—preserve the birds instead of killing them for their plumage.

Baynes came to Meriden to study wildlife in the nearby Corbin Preserve and teach at Kimbal Academy. Enthusiastic and persuasive, he talked the townspeople and students into making Meriden a haven for birds. *Choice White Pines and Good Land: A History of Plainfield and Meriden*, written by fifty-six residents and sold now through local libraries, recounts the fascinating history of Baynes's Bird Club from its inception in 1911.

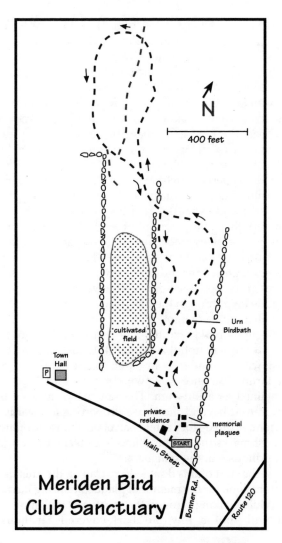

N

400 feet

Town
Hall

P

cultivated
field

Urn
Birdbath

private
residence

memorial
plaques

START

Main Street

Bonner Rd.

Route 120

Meriden Bird
Club Sanctuary

All sorts of work went into protecting birds. The town blacksmith redesigned flour and sugar barrels into four-story birdhouses placed on poles (like the one seen at the entrance to the sanctuary). Students trampled snow around numerous feeding stations during winter so ground birds could forage for food. Discarded Christmas trees were decorated with suet bags. And the Audubon Bird House Company turned out 150 copies of a popular German birdhouse, fabricating them from logs with natural bark on the exterior.

This property, purchased with a bequest from Helen Woodruff Smith, was an abandoned farm of sloping pasture and meadowland skirted by woods. A 1938 guide mentions that "bird houses of every type hang from trees, and drinking pools are numerous amid the ferns. Bird baths are placed at intervals." The meadows have long since grown in, and fewer pools and birdbaths are seen as you follow the upper and then the lower sides of a double loop through the thirty-two-acre sanctuary. But the walk is still a delight.

Begin by parking at the Meriden Town Hall lot and walk to the left uphill less than 0.1 mile past a large house with a stone masonry arch to one side. This private farmhouse once was owned by the Bird Club and maintained as a museum. The sanctuary entrance has been moved beyond the house property a few yards to the right. A three-story white barrel birdhouse topping a tall post marks the trailhead and is emblematic of original birdhouses at the sanctuary.

At the start of this double-loop trail on the hillside to the right, look for the memorial plaque honoring Baynes.

While walking through the sanctuary, look high and you will spot a few old bark-covered birdhouses

An urn birdbath designed by Augustus Saint-Gaudens and presented at the dedication of the sanctuary in 1913.

attached to the sturdier trees. Although unblazed, the trail is worn and wide most of the way. At the first Y junction, veer right. A brush pile centered on a ground cover of shiny-leaved periwinkle probably has been left as a refuge for birds and small forest dwellers during ice and snowstorms.

For about 0.3 mile, your walk parallels a stone wall on the right.

Beneath large sugar maple and white pine grow two-foot-tall gentians with blue funneled starlike flowers and smooth opposite leaves. In the dappled sunlight appear the showy magenta blossoms of flowering raspberry. In the fall their thimbleberries attract birds, though humans prefer true raspberries.

Shortly, you arrive at a clearing with a bench and an ornate bronze urn birdbath designed by Augusta Saint-Gaudens and dedicated in the amphitheater on this site in 1913. Judging from the imaginative bas relief around the birdbath pedestal, it's easy to see that the famous Cornish sculptor Augustus Saint-Gaudens married a talented artist. Ernest Baynes, the daughters of President Woodrow Wilson, and others from the Cornish Colony donned bird masks and wings to perform "Sanctuary," a masque written by Percy MacKaye to commemorate the inception of the sanctuary.

One of the three original birdbaths chiseled from boulders weighing several tons has been removed to the "green" at the Kimbal Academy in the center of Plainfield. Though the birdbath is drilled and fitted with a conduit for water, the shallow bowl contained only dust the day we saw it. Augusta's birdbath did have water, albeit a bit murky from leaf litter from the deciduous trees overhead.

Continue on the upper half of the loop through woods dotted with white birch. Phoebes and chickadees chatter and call "fee-bee," indistinguishable at times (at other times the chickadee's "chick-a-dee-dee-dee" is definitive). Black-capped chickadees are smaller, with black head and throat and buff-colored sides, and are rotund; the tail-wagging, fly-catching phoebes are gray and slimmer.

For about a hundred yards the wall on your right disappears. Then at 0.3 mile you pass through an opening in another stone wall. Keep to the right and walk downhill on the duff trail through deciduous forest. At the Y junction, again keep to the right.

The next junction at 0.6 mile brings you to the far edge of the property. At this X junction, with you at the center, veer left on the upper arm of the X.

Walk downhill to the lower part of the double loop, passing two fine yellow birch on the right. "Yellow" birch is the official name but the bronze-gold color of the bark is unmistakable. This birch winters over well and is the hardiest of the northern birches. It also is one of the most useful timber trees, often substituted for hard maple or pine. A few paces beyond the birch are two tall straight white ash trees, their bark gray and ridged (they grow with a broad crown if out in the open). Identified by pointed, oval, opposite leaflets in clusters of seven (dark green on top, silvery beneath), this tree also is a valuable lumber tree because of the durability of the wood.

A few more paces on and to the left, note the natural birdhouse blending in with the dark bark of a huge hemlock tree.

Veer left when you arrive at a visible cross trail. Continue straight ahead and uphill. For a few hundred feet you will be retracing your steps, returning to the opening in the stone wall. But this time, directly after passing through the opening, turn right and walk along the stone wall through mature white birch and pine forest.

At 1.1 miles step across mossy stones in a rivulet whose source is an invisible natural spring. Once more the trail reverts to pine needles. Beyond the wall pasture pines grow at the edge of a field.

At 1.2 miles note the good-sized snag (a standing barkless dead tree). Snags provide excellent habitat for red squirrel, owls, and other forest creatures. Woodpeckers and nuthatches drill holes in them for fast-food stops. As the holes widen, they in turn provide shelter for spiders, bats, and a variety of other lodgers.

On your right an owl house is attached to a venerable old sugar maple. A few paces farther a tote road comes in from the right. Veer left onto the wide tote road and traverse the initial periwinkle-carpeted clearing. At 1.3 miles you will recognize the original Y junction. Continue another 0.1 mile to the Bird Sanctuary entrance.

Here you may relax on a bench among the lovely landscaped flowerbeds. In 1978 sixty bluebird houses built by members of the 4-H Club were distributed throughout the town by the Meriden Bird Club. If you're lucky, you might glimpse a bluebird, hummingbird, or butterfly among the colorful blossoms.

Today, more than 200 communities across the country support bird sanctuaries. Their existence is due in large part to the vision of Ernest Baynes, Helen Woodruff Smith, and the care and concern Meriden residents have demonstrated for almost a century on behalf of their feathered friends.

Getting There

From I-89 take Exit 18 at Lebanon, turning south on NH 120. Drive approximately 8 miles and turn right onto Main Street in Meriden. Park at the Meriden Town Hall on the right.

Coming from Saint-Gaudens (see p. 216) on NH 12A, drive north to Plainfield. You may pick up a Bird Sanctuary map at the Plainfield Public Library. Across from the library is Daniels Road. Take it to Stage Road, turn right and drive about 5 miles to NH 120 north. Turn left. Make another left turn onto Main Street in Meriden. Park in the lot at the Meriden Town Hall.

Other Information

To Frenches Ledges Trail, drive downhill from the Meriden Town Hall on Main Street, cross a covered bridge, and turn left on Columbus Jordan Road. This is a favorite local spot.

Saint-Gaudens National Historic Site

Blow-Me-Up Ravine Trail (Loop)
Cornish

- **0.3 mile**
- **20 minutes**
- **easy**

An old cart path into a deep ravine and along picturesque Blow-Me-Up River.

In 1892 renowned sculptor Augustus Saint-Gaudens bought an estate near the Connecticut River in Cornish, New Hampshire. In front of the Federal-style, 200-year-old brick residence stands a massive, thornless honey locust planted by Saint-Gaudens more than a century ago. He converted the old barn into his studio and named the residence Aspet after his father's birthplace in France. Artistic friends who visited and summered with the popular sculptor bought neighboring estates with grand views of Mount Ascutney in Vermont, and soon Cornish had a flourishing artist colony.

Skirt your way to the left of the main residence (now a museum), passing the Doric-columned arcade of the pergola (a long, ramada-like trellis with vines growing overhead). Continue through a formal flower garden of

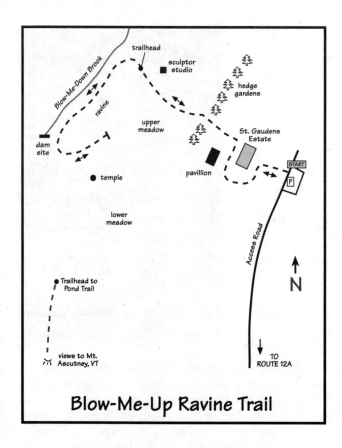

Blow-Me-Up Ravine Trail

old-fashioned perennials. As you make your way past classical Greek columns, marble pools, and statues of Pan, you might agree with one of the guests that the estate resembles an "upright New England farmer with a new set of false teeth."

This common Christmas fern is found on rocky, wooded hillsides and is named after the pinnae that are somewhat shaped like Christmas stockings.

Many of the gardens in Cornish were designed by Ellen Shipman (while her husband, Louis, wrote plays). Behind the house the tradition continues with an extensive flower garden where annuals are grown to replenish the many flower beds on the grounds.

Enter the Adams Memorial garden and pass on your right a copy of a bronze sculpture that was commissioned by historian Henry Adams in memory of his wife, Clover. Adams called the sculpture *The Peace of God;* Saint-Gaudens titled it *The Mystery of the Hereafter ...beyond pain and beyond joy.*

Immediately through an arch in the high hedge is an alleyway of birch trees. Ensconced in the woods directly across the lawn (which Saint-Gaudens once used as a bowling green) are Ravine Studio and the barely visible trailhead.

Originally the studio housed Saint-Gaudens' marble cutters. But after a fire destroyed his studio in 1904, along with many sketches and notes, he moved in. Currently, guest sculptors are often in residence, so keep noise to a minimum as you enter the woods to the left of Ravine Studio.

Trail identifications begin directly behind the sign Ravine Trail. If brochures aren't available for the nine-stop trail, the self-guided identifications refer to the following:

1. Glaciers, rain, and streams have worn away the land, creating this steep chasm. Watch your step as you descend the ravine on what once was a cart path. Now a well-maintained walkway negotiates the steep slope to a brook below.

2. On your right is a huge decaying tree trunk. Shallow-rooted trees often tumble, fall, and decay, adding nutrients to the forest floor and providing food for insects and a host of other organisms. We identified several incredibly odd and colorful mushrooms, including sunburst-colored shelf mushrooms, orange mycena looking like miniature cocktail parasols atop a log, and the sometimes phallic looking dog stinkhorn, named for its often offensive odor. Bring your mushroom guidebook.

3. The brook burbles along in the dappled sunlight through a natural garden of ferns. This ravine is a fern

The moist, dark ravine provides good habitat for mushrooms like this yellow-orange fan-shaped chicken mushroom, which grows stalkless, fusing to trees at the base.

identifier's paradise. The dark green earth-hugging ferns with shiny stocking-shaped leaves are Christmas ferns; they are evergreen, and you'll find them poking through the snow all winter. Wood, or shield, ferns have triangular leaves along the stipe (central stem). Tall cinnamon ferns bear a single rust brown fertile frond containing spore cases and sometimes grow to five feet.

4. The original stream through the western part of Cornish was called Blomidon, which locals translated to Blow-Me-Down. Amused by this name, artists at the colony dubbed this branch of the river Blow-Me-Up.

5. Look for evergreen trees with soft, short, flat needles and small cones. The boughs of hemlock furnish protected deer yards during winter storms.

6. In this ravine grow some of the tallest eastern white pine we've ever seen (100 feet, possibly more). In colonial times fabulously tall, straight, strong pines were marked with a special symbol; these "King's pines" were used for masts on eighteenth-century English warships. White pine needles three to four inches long come in bunches of five.

7. Deciduous woods in New Hampshire often are comprised of oak, beech, and maple. Along the brook yellow birch are recognized easily by their shiny bronze-gold bark.

8. Turn to the right and stand on the footbridge spanning the rushing brook. Here you can examine slate and phyllites compressed from the primordial ooze of an ancient inland sea. Downstream you can see the remains of a field-stone dam used as a swimming hole that Saint-Gaudens built for his assistants, colonist friends, and himself. During spring, thunderclouds billow over Mount Ascutney to the west and shower this brook, sending torrents into the nearby Connecticut River. When the Connecticut crests, farm folk in the fertile river valley are evacuated and low-lying farm fields are completely flooded.

Loop to your left now and climb steadily back toward the light of the open sky above the lawn.

9. As you near the top of the ravine, listen. The woods are alive with birdsong, burbling water, chattering chipmunks, a zephyr blowing through the pine boughs. Actually, listening is always a good idea whenever and

wherever you're in the woods. Open your ears as you do your eyes for a symphony of natural sounds.

To the right of the trail terminus in the meadow is the setting for a masque (pageant) performed in 1905 to celebrate the twentieth anniversary of the Cornish Colony. Today, the marble "temple" marks the burial site of the Saint-Gaudens family. The two-mile Blow-Me-Down Pond Trail enters the woods at the far end of the meadow to the right.

Getting There

From I-89 in West Lebanon take Exit 20 onto NH 12A south (along the Connecticut River) for 12 miles to the Saint-Gaudens prominent sign on your left. Drive 0.6 mile up the access road to the parking lot on the right.

From the junction of NH 103 west outside Claremont, drive on NH 12A north 12 miles to the prominent Saint-Gaudens sign on your right. Drive 0.6 mile up the access road to the parking lot on the right.

Other Information

Saint-Gaudens National Historic Site
R.R. 3 Box 73
Cornish, NH 03745-9704
603-675-2175

Nominal fee for adults over sixteen. Senior passes acknowledged. Tour of Saint-Gaudens estate and house.

Nearby canoe rentals on the Connecticut River; several covered bridges in the area.

Saint-Gaudens National Historic Site

Blow-Me-Down Pond Trail (Loop)

Cornish

- **2 miles**
- **1 hour**
- **moderate to difficult**

A delightful excursion downward through spacious mixed woods to a sycamore grove, a stone-arch bridge, and an old woolen mill, and back upward to the cleared fields of the Saint-Gaudens residence.

After perhaps touring the main house, studios, and grounds, enjoy the long, gentle slope of the field and the sweeping view in front of the main residence museum (also now park headquarters). The trailhead is located at the far end of the field beyond the "temple" in sight to the right.

To get there, walk from the Saint-Gaudens residence and along the right-hand edge of the woods (you'll pass the exit of the Ravine Trail). A sign indicating the trailhead of the Blow-Me-Down Pond Trail is visible from the temple, a white marble replica of a pillared facade of a Greek temple where the remains of the Augustus Saint-Gaudens family rest.

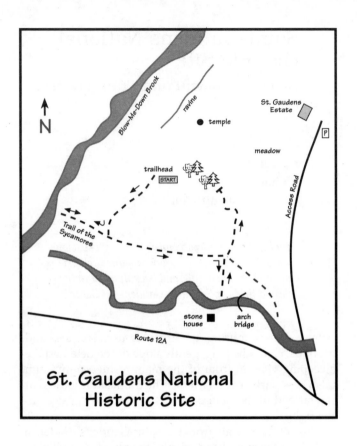

St. Gaudens National Historic Site

As you approach a downward bank of the field past the temple, notice how the woods in the distance turn at a sharp left angle where the field ends. About a third of the way across the edge of the woods, you can see a dark gap in the tree line. This is the entrance to the trail.

The long first section of a gradual descent takes you on a log-lined path through airy woods. The trail isn't blazed but is well worn. These are pleasant woods. Giant American beech trees especially are noticeable for their relatively slender giraffe-like trunks because of stretching so high in competition for sunlight. Thick white-pine trunks with rugged black bark grow left and right of you. These plentiful giant pines are the reason this area was called the Mastlands—it was a source of masts for the British Royal Navy in pre-Revolutionary days.

In 0.1 mile after entering the woods, the terrain flattens. In another 100 feet a log bench on your right makes a good resting spot as well as a place to identify some of the ferns surrounding you. The ostrich fern is plentiful along this trail and can be recognized in full summer growth by its long (up to 5 feet) plumelike fronds that are tapered top and bottom.

The rich, moist soil underfoot is also a good place to look for lycopodium club mosses. In this pine-dense forest, club mosses are deceiving. They look like evergreen saplings on their way to growing into 100-foot timbers. These five-to-six-inch-high lycopods may appear like miniature pine trees but, in fact, they are growing from subterranean running stems, or rhizome systems. The so-called bristly club moss grows singly and looks like an upright short-needled spruce twig. The tree club moss and its relative, the running pine, look like tiny pine trees. Club moss is also called ground cedar. These very ancient plants aren't mosses but spore-bearing plants (true mosses lack vessels in their stems to move water and nutrients along, hence their inability to grow tall).

In about 0.4 mile the main trail meets a junction (the log-lined pathway ends here). A sign indicates Trail of the Sycamores to the right. Dead-ending at Blow-Me-Down Brook, this slightly descending side trail totals 0.3 mile round-trip back to the junction. Take it.

This spur trail stops abruptly at the bank of the brook, where a bench to the right overlooks three or four American sycamores from a once larger stand. These elegant trees are members of the ancient plane tree family, traced to the Mesozoic age—the time of the dinosaurs. They're identified first of all by their smooth, mottled, whitish bark spotted with tan patches. The other two markers are the prickly buttonballs covered with tiny spikes and webbed, maple-like leaves. Sycamores like water and often line streams such as this in a country setting.

Return on the Sycamore Trail to the junction sign and proceed straight on the Return Trail, continuing ahead toward new territory. (The sign is somewhat confusing; this is one of several Return Trail junctions.)

Continue on the Blow-Me-Down Pond Trail to the pond, which lies another 0.5 mile farther.

The trail may muddy your boots a bit, but nothing above your instep. As you proceed, there are four footbridges to help you over the soggy areas. They're sturdy and well built; one has a handrail and the others are well placed barkless split logs.

The closer the trail to Blow-Me-Down Pond on the right, the more inlets and outlets are negotiated. In 0.2 mile a grand old stone mill building appears through the thick maple and birch branches. Soon the mill appears in full view on the right directly opposite you on the trail. The trail then slants downward to a small roadside field.

This stone mill built in 1830 processed sheep wool.

At this point make a hairpin turn and proceed down the short steep road to the pond, where you can see the water rushing over the dam and the mill up close. This mill was operated by Walter Mercer in the 1830s and processed wool supplied by local shepherds (a century ago New Hampshire was only about 15 percent forested, not the 85 percent of today; much of the land was sheep-grazing pasture).

Be sure to look for a picturesque stone arch bridge half-hidden to your left across the stream as you start down the access road/ramp to the dam. It's a beauty.

Unless you walk onto NH 12A, you won't be able to read the historic marker at the mill site. Here's what it says:

> The Cornish Colony (1883–1935) was a group of artists, sculptors, writers, journalists, poets, and musicians who joined the sculptor Augustus Saint-Gaudens in Cornish and found the area a delightful place to live and work. Some prominent members were sculptor Herbert Adams, poet Percy MacKaye, architect Charles A. Platt, artists Kenyon Cox, Stephen Parrish and his son Maxfield, and landscape architects Rose Nichols and Ellen Shipman.

Continuing the walk, return up the pond access ramp and make the hairpin turn in reverse to get back onto the woods trail. Since your attention was probably on the mill building when you arrived, now is the time to look for horsetail plant, barberry shrub, and sensitive fern.

A cluster of hollow, segmented horsetail grows by the side of the trail. The plant grows in thin, brittle, green stalks straight upward. Curiously, horsetail is related to the fern family even though it looks like a relative of bamboo.

Barberry bushes, with their thorny network of switchlike stems and teardrop-shaped leaves, produce drooping red berries high on the plant. Most often, these plants are reminders of civilization—growing near abandoned house and mill sites. Look for sensitive ferns, too, along here. Their wide chartreuse fronds seem hardy, but in reality they fold up and wither at the first touch of fall frost, hence their name.

In 0.2 mile from the pond turn right at the first junction for the Return Trail. Cross a footbridge over a small brook culvert right away and climb the trail.

The distance from the pond to the end of the trail at the field edge is 0.5 mile (with the same bench at the forest exit).

With the temple now on your left across the field, walk along the edge of the woods on the right side of the field toward Aspet and the parking lot.

Getting There

From I-89 in West Lebanon, take Exit 20 on NH 12A south (along the Connecticut River) for 12 miles to the prominent Saint-Gaudens sign on your left. Drive 0.6 mile on the access road to the parking lot on the right.

From the junction of NH 103 west outside Claremont, drive on NH 12A north 12 miles to the prominent Saint-Gaudens sign on the right. Drive 0.6 mile on the access road to the parking lot on the right.

Other Information

Saint-Gaudens National Historic Site
R.R. 3 Box 73
Cornish, NH 03745-9704
603-675-2175

Charlestown Conservation Area

Claybrook Nature Trail

Charlestown

- 0.75 mile
- 40 minutes
- easy

A riverine trail winding and descending through hemlock and hardwoods.

The dramatic rush of the brook cascading through a deep ravine turns later into a wide, gentle flowing stream. The trail parallels the brook nearly all the way, making this walk a memorable woodland stroll.

The trail begins at a small hummock of earth beside the road about ten yards to the left of an old dam on Clay Brook. Cross through a sumac-dotted field for 100 feet to a white sign prohibiting vehicular traffic and enter the hemlock forest. The trail, established on private land made available by Mrs. Doris Bacon and William Manning, is maintained by the Charlestown Conservation Commission. Please respect the nature around you. Pack out what you pack in and stay on the trail.

Though unblazed, a clearly visible path parallels the river for the entire walk. Very soon after entering the

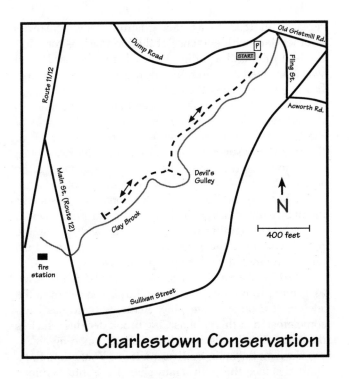

Charlestown Conservation

evergreens, make a 25-foot detour on your left to the edge of deeply chiseled Devil's Gulley. (Hold tightly to smaller children's hands; the drop to the river bottom plummets more than 100 feet). Here Clay Brook cascades down from the old dam upriver at the road and through this deep narrow gorge, eventually debouching into the nearby Connecticut River. An old sawmill once was located on the east side of Devil's Gulley and on the west side, a stone gristmill originally built in 1744 was replaced in 1833 by another gristmill. Downstream is another dam with evidence of the foundations for a linseed-oil mill, and a fulling mill, where processed wool was thickened by carefully adding moisture and then heating and pressing the material.

Back on the main trail, descend another 0.1 mile. To the left and below near the riverbank is the stone wall of the grist-mill. Keep on descending. Farther on the left of the trail tower several giant oaks. A high Norway pine, also known as red pine, presents a close-up view of its square shields of ruddy bark. Some of the older pines along here are riddled with holes bored by sapsuckers intent on extracting sap and insects from the punky wood.

After descending through a white-birch grove, the path levels near the riverbed, where in summer lush ferns and tangled wild grapes proliferate.

At 0.25 mile a short switchback to the left leads down to a river promontory and a delightful picnic spot in the shelter of a huge white pine. Actually, there has been some erosion at this spot as Clay Brook decides which is the path of least resistance during spring flooding.

Back on the main trail, veer left at a Y junction. For a short distance the path again shies back into hemlock forest.

In a clearing of saplings, a rivulet cuts away from Clay Brook and skirts the trail. In this clay riverbed, cinnamon ferns spread their plumes from the center outward like chartreuse fountains in the mossy outcrops along the shale riverbank. Take time to feel the soft hairs that grow along the majestic stems of these luxuriant two-foot fronds.

All members of the woodpecker family from the large pileated woodpecker to the tiny yellow-bellied sapsucker drill trees for insects and sap, leaving burrows for other forest creatures.

The walk dead-ends at the river across from the stone remains of a washed-out bridge. The highway overpass looms straight ahead. A footbridge is being planned for walkers to cross the river to finish their walk at the Charlestown fire station where the historic district starts, thus linking the urban and nature walks.

Early spring might be the best time for this walk, before the black flies arrive and when spring runoff enhances the crashing cascade spilling and rilling through the woods. Children over ten certainly will thrill to the drama of the water, and parents can tone their hibernating muscles on the steady, gradual climb back to the road.

Getting There

Drive north on NH 12 through Charlestown to Sullivan Street prior to the fire station. Turn right on Sullivan and drive 0.7 mile. Turn left on Fling Road (Acworth Road is to the right). Drive the 0.2-mile connector (Fling Road), crossing the bridge and turning left onto Old Grist Mill Road. Park immediately on the left of Old Grist Mill Road near the Clay Brook dam.

Other Information

Charlestown Historic District
Main Street
Charlestown, NH 03603
603-826-4400

Historic Charlestown Walkabout is a guide booklet that tells about the buildings on Main Street, the early mills on Clay Brook, the museum at Fort #4, Crown Point Road markers (on the 1760 road from the Fort #4 to Crown Point on Lake Champlain), and other points of interest.

For information about trails along the Connecticut River write to:

Joint Rivers Commission
P.O. Box 1182
Charlestown, NH 03603

Daniel Webster Birthplace State Historic Site

Daniel Webster Nature Trail (Loop)

Franklin

- **0.5 mile**
- **20 minutes**
- **easy**

A saunter through spacious woods down to
Punch Brook and back up a small old farm field
fronting the two-room home where the renowned
"Defender of the Constitution" was born.

The boy who became the great American statesman and orator once walked the same ground here as you. Daniel Webster (1782–1852) was born in the small house featured at this state historic site. An extraordinary man, he was secretary of state under Presidents William Henry Harrison, John Tyler, and Millard Fillmore; ran for the presidency as a leader of a faction of the Whig Party in 1836; served for years as U.S. representative for New Hampshire; and, after moving to Massachusetts, was congressman and later senator from that state.

The nature trail circles through the woods that surround a hillside field where his father, Ebenezer Webster, settled about 1775 along what was a former Indian trail

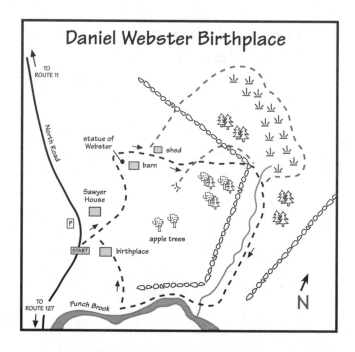

Daniel Webster Birthplace

TO
ROUTE 11

North Road

statue of
Webster

shed

barn

Sawyer
House

P

apple trees

START   birthplace

TO
ROUTE 127

Punch Brook

N

to Canada. At one point Ebenezer Webster was thought
to be the northernmost white in the area.

The fourth child of Ebenezer and Abigail Webster,
Daniel astounded his elders and teachers with his
knowledge and memorization of the Bible and works of
English literature. Although a feeble child himself, he
inherited his father's sense of drama and his mother's
love of reading.

Later in life when he opened a law practice in
Marshfield, Massachusetts, he said of New Hampshire,
"For my part, I shall continue to love her white-topped

hills, her clear running streams, her beautiful lakes, and her deep shady forests as long as I live."

Although the trailhead into some of these deep shady forests begins officially behind the Webster birth site, we recommend starting at the end point so that the walk is mostly downhill.

From the front of the park building on the left, walk uphill and veer diagonally to the left of the field toward the left-hand corner of the barn (this former dairy barn was built in 1930 and in the 1970s was converted to a local stage theater and restaurant). You'll pass by a wooden statue of Daniel Webster by New Hampshire chainsaw artist Tom Worcester. The work depicts the well-known orator in a no-nonsense pose as the "Defender of the Constitution" who proclaimed to historic memory, "The Union, one and inseparable, now and forever."

Circle around the rear of the barn and pass between it and the storage shed, turn left, and walk in front of the shed as you proceed up toward the corner of the woods and field ahead.

Enter the woods at the left-hand corner of the field where the trail appears. No blazes are necessary; the trail is clearly worn. You're at the high point of the trail; the rest is level or downhill walking.

Fifteen feet into the woods look for low-lying examples of Canada lily, a flowering plant with three broad leaves and hanging white hooded flowers on a stalk. The surprise of this flower comes when you lift up the hanging blossoms to see the shy bright-orange coloring inside. You'd never know otherwise.

In the next 100 feet low-lying creeper partridgeberry plants are plentiful, with their two pinkish flowers that turn into two bright red berries.

The woods are spacious. Great white pine grow here, their thick trunks dominating eye-level views, their five-needle clusters padding the trail and helping to keep the woods quiet. Open woods like these offer welcome chances of seeing ground-loving plants, especially the "blushers" and "tawny milkcap" mushrooms: red-toned, saucer-shaped fungi widespread in pine and mixed forests.

Look, too, for the easily identified Indian pipe. Ghostly white from stem to flowers, the plant is also known as corpse plant and ghost flower. Indian pipe is white because the plant lacks chlorophyll. Because of this, it cannot get energy from sunlight; it receives nourishment from decayed vegetable matter in the soil. Indian pipes stand in individual stalks not much taller than a half-foot high with waxlike hanging hooded blossoms. They turn brown at the end of the season.

Cross a thin brook that in early spring drains into Punch Brook below but dries up in summer. Follow the trail as it bends to the right.

Continue downhill alongside the brook now on your right for 200 feet, cross it, and then curve right with the larger Punch Brook on the left.

Here at 0.3 mile the woodland growth by the trail flourishes into giant ferns. The pathway narrows and forces you to brush by prime examples of waist-high interrupted ferns. Also known as Clayton's fern, the fronds of the interrupted fern sometimes grow five feet long and measure a foot wide. Water loving and widespread, interrupted fern is seen, too, in moist woodlands and along open fields. Its reproductive spores grow in microscopic sacs on shriveled brownish pinnae in the middle of one or two of the fronds, thus "interrupting" a frond.

Continue ahead for thirty feet before ascending slightly and passing between two giant white pines, probably 150 years old (as estimated by park guide Don Fitts). In early spring, he said, the tall, brilliant red cardinal flowers brighten the resurrecting woods here.

Turn right and enter the clearing behind Daniel Webster's birthplace.

On the right in the field, two ancient apple trees grow, illustrating an intriguing arboreal history. As Fitts explains it, Ebenezer Webster planted the trees in the late 1700s at the top of the field. As apples fell off the trees

The birthplace of Daniel Webster.

The stemless lady-slipper is a relatively common orchid with a purplish pouch (or slipper) found in pine-dominated forests.

and rolled downhill, seeds took root. Then as the trees died, gravity felled them downhill, too. Meanwhile, the seeds that took root grew into mature trees. This process continued, regrowing sets of trees progressively down the field. The downhill chain continued through the generations until the pair of apple trees now standing at the bottom of the field are the latest descendants of the orchards.

Another tree development is happening on the site. A pair of eight-year-old American Liberty elm trees planted here are now reaching thirty feet in height, a sign that the graceful trees may be surviving into maturity. This is part of a continuing project of resurrecting the beloved, fountainlike elm that was felled by Dutch elm disease in the early twentieth century. A special fungicide developed through the Elm Research Institute in Harrisville, New Hampshire, is being distributed and applied to elm trees by "conscientious injectors," as those in the national network of people trying to bring back the elms are called. More than 250,000 American Liberty elms have been distributed nationwide since 1983.

Continue walking upward past the Webster house to the parking area.

Getting There

From US 3/NH 11 west in Franklin, turn onto US 3/NH 127 west (left). Drive 0.6 mile, turn south (right) at the Daniel Webster sign and continue to follow NH 127. After 0.2 mile turn right again onto North Road (at the next Daniel Webster sign). Drive 2.1 miles and turn right at the next sign onto North Road. (This road has no road sign but the state sign to the Daniel Webster Birthplace is well marked.) Drive 0.7 mile on this road and park to the left across from the Webster cabin.

Other Information

Hours: Open weekends and holidays mid-May to late June; daily through Labor Day; weekends only through Columbus Day.

No fee for the trail. Small fee to tour the birthplace.

Franklin Falls Dam

New Hampshire Heritage & Franklin Dam Trail (U.S. Army Corps of Engineers)

Franklin

- **1.8 miles**
- **1 hour**
- **moderate (with one short steep section)**

An enticing tidbit of New Hampshire's 230-mile,
state-long Heritage Trail (in progress) joins a connector
trail to the Franklin Falls Dam and Reservoir
on the Pemigewasset River.

The New Hampshire Heritage Trail is a countryside corridor running the length of the Granite State, from Massachusetts to Canada. Since the first section of the planned 230-mile trail was dedicated in Franconia Notch in 1989, new sections have been added. These sections eventually will be linked to others that will pass along the Merrimack, Pemigewasset, and Connecticut Rivers as well as local towns en route.

This walk to the Franklin Falls Dam includes sections of the Heritage Trail. Enter the grounds by the gate. The park-hours sign has a yellow blaze on it.

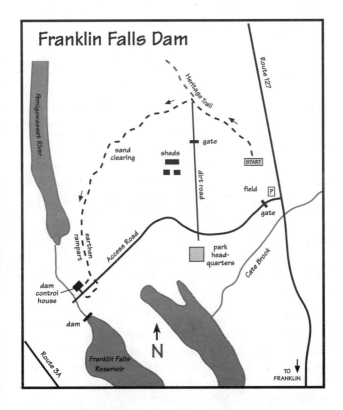

Franklin Falls Dam

Route 127

Heritage Trail

gate

sand clearing

sheds

dirt road

START

field P

gate

earthen rampart

Access Road

park head-quarters

Cate Brook

dam control house

Pemigewasset River

dam

Route 3A

Franklin Falls Reservoir

N

TO FRANKLIN

Follow the mowed meadow path on the right of the asphalt entrance road and walk between two strangely located birdhouses on tall posts. In spring, swallow fledglings occupy these birdhouses and flustered parents divebomb walkers who linger too long to gawk at their cute, ravenous offspring (see p. 240).

About six yards from the meadow, a prominent Heritage Trail sign points walkers into a forested area of white pines. Walk down the slope through a clearing and turn right on the wide, grassy, needle-strewn trail. The wind soughs through the pine boughs. Long six- to eight-inch pine cones littering the trail confirm the proximity of stately white pines common in New Hampshire.

Pass a shed off the trail on the left. At 0.2 mile veer right; abruptly you're on a gravel bank lined with gray birch. These short trees are nicknamed "poverty birches" because they seem to proliferate on abandoned farmland and poor soil. The small arrow-shaped leaves are much more pointed than those of the white birch.

This completely blazed section of the Heritage Trail eventually drops into the Pemigewasset River valley, coming out at an old mill site on Salmon Brook. (A flier for the Franklin-to-Sanbornton northbound section of the Heritage Trail may be picked up at the headquarters.) However, the Franklin Dam is the objective of this walk.

At 0.4 mile, a Heritage Trail sign on the left of the trail points to a connector trail from the west side of the dam. Turn left on the sand road and walk a few paces. Then take the narrower tote road that bears to the right. (Look for the yellow blaze on a pine tree to the right at 0.5 mile.)

This area is a sand moraine, a legacy of the Ice Age, and walking across it is like traversing a minidesert. A few hardy gray birch provide scant shade, and the equally hardy sweet fern exudes its fragrance, especially in the blazing sun.

Although the frondy two-foot-high sweet fern resembles a fern, it's not; unlike the fern, it prefers dry impoverished soil and is really a member of the bayberry family. Because it often grows in nutrient-deficient barren wastelands such as this, it depends on bacteria (actinomycetes) to help it acquire nitrogen. This symbiotic relationship in turn provides the bacteria a home on the plant's root system. Some herbalists claim the leaves of sweet fern make a tasty tea. They don't, in our opinion, and in any case you'll want to leave this fern where it is so others may enjoy its fragrance.

In spite of the lack of vegetation here, deer-hoof prints are in evidence along the trail. Maybe the deer were on their way, in the soft, protective light of dawn or dusk, to the river to drink.

Opposite the yellow blaze on a post to the left, a lone white pine uncharacteristically has branches that come off the trunk very close to the ground. Ordinarily, you'd expect a white pine to be rather spindly for its first several feet above ground, with few branches. But unlike the magnificent stand of white pine towering in the distance high into the sky, this loner has no competitors for sunlight. Therefore, it has comfortably branched out in all directions like a huge bushy Christmas tree.

At another post with a blaze bear left, climbing about ten yards onto an embankment (0.65 mile) that is part of the rampart for the dam and flood control. The ridge has been planted with several ornamental trees. Note the several species of spruce on the left of the trail. Spruce are identified easily. Evergreen, they have short stiff needles prickly to the touch. (Short-needled hemlock and fir are much softer.) Think "sharp spruce" and "friendly fir." White spruce (*Picea glauca*) is blue-green and used for erosion control on sites like this embankment. Its cousin, the Norway spruce, grows twenty feet taller (to ninety feet), and has drooping graceful boughs.

A baby swallow waits for a feeding.

Watch your step descending the rampart to the asphalt access road at 0.8 mile. Turn right, following the blazes that continue on the guardrail posts across the high levee to the control tower. The granite rocks used for fill are embedded with sparkling flecks of mirrorlike mica, black grains of schist, and white quartz crystals. This amalgam of igneous rock fused and solidified by volcanic activity millions of years ago is what gives the Granite State its name, and here there's literally a mountain of it.

In 1936 the Merrimack River flooded, destroying homes and bridges in Concord, Manchester, and as far south as Lawrence and Lowell, Massachusetts. Congress authorized the U.S. Army Corps of Engineers to construct a system of dams along the Merrimack and other river basins of New England. The Franklin Dam was built in 1943. Located above the Merrimack River on the Pemigewasset, which runs through 2,500 wooded acres of white pine, oak, maple, beech, and birch, the dam services a large drainage area of 1,000 square miles of neighboring mountains and snowmelt torrents channeled into an extensive watershed. Because the river flows through the dam unobstructed in mild conditions, the basin usually is relatively dry, except when the river crests and during threatening flood conditions. Nevertheless, walkers enjoy a glorious view of the river valley from this high vantage point.

Along with the joggers and bikers, you can return to the trailhead via the park access road to the parking lot. We prefer going back the way we came. Somehow, what you see on the way always looks different in reverse.

Getting There

From I-93 north of Concord, take Exit 22. Turn south (right) on NH 127 and drive 3.3 miles to the reservoir entrance gate (Federal Dam Access Road) and asphalt parking area to the right. Park here. The gate is open 7:00 A.M. to 3:30 P.M. and leads to the trailhead.

Other Information

U.S. Army Corps of Engineers/New England
Franklin Falls Dam
46 Granite Drive
Franklin, NH 03235-2202
603-934-2116

Hiking also at Blackwater Dam off NH 3A at Webster. Call Hal Graham 603-286-3506 for up-to-date information on the New Hampshire Heritage Trail.

Sanbornton I-93 Rest Area

Sanbornton Boulder Nature Trail (Loop)

Sanbornton

- **0.3 mile**
- **20 minutes**
- **easy**

Several delightful discoveries await leg-stretching drivers at this I-93 rest area, including one of the largest free-standing boulders in New Hampshire.

A nature walk at a highway rest area? Why not! Even busy travelers passing through can take a break and learn a little about New England's landscape on this quick nature walk.

"Welcome to our Rest Area" reads a large sign at the top of a flight of steps to the right of the building. "We invite you to stretch your legs on our self-guiding Nature Trail. New Hampshire forests are important to you for recreation, wood products, clear water, and air. Our trail will lead you to natural happenings that put you in touch with the resources around you."

Pick up a flier for the trail at the rest-area information desk if none is in the box to the side of the trailhead. To the left and a few feet from the stairs is a marker post

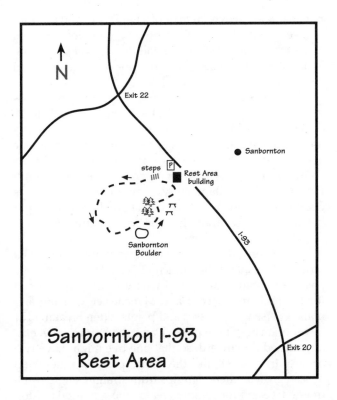

Sanbornton I-93
Rest Area

with a powder blue blaze and white arrow. Though many of the eleven numbered stakes were missing when we were there, with a little searching it is amazing how much you'll discover near this busy public area.

Climbing the gentle slope, for instance, look for miniature "ground pines," also called "ground cedar" (stop 2). These club mosses, smaller than Japanese bonsai but no less attractive, are part of a family of plants 50 million years old. Lowly as they grow now, millions of years ago such plants stretched as tall as 100 feet in the air. Today the club mosses that carpet the forest floor are on New Hampshire's protected list.

Lichen are another curious low-lying growth. As you pass granite boulders ahead, notice the leaflike lichen attached to the stone surfaces. These organisms are symbiotic combinations of fungi and photosynthetic green algae or blue-green bacteria. Lichen grow virtually everywhere, even underwater and near the South Pole. Now that's adaptability. They soften on rainy days because they absorb up to 35 percent of their own weight in water, turn green, and lose the brittle texture that most of us associate with them.

At the turn of the century, Mr. Sanbornton owned a farm and this land, like much of New Hampshire, was pasture for cattle and sheep whose wool was destined for the mills in Concord and Manchester. Grazing animals browsed the grasses and plants, often breaking the lower branches of the pines. Damaged branches eventually turned downward, so that one tree might have two or three trunks to it, like the white "pasture" pines (stop 3) seen growing here. Stumps from straight single-trunk trees harvested for lumber create "moss mounds" (stop 4), hummocks of decayed wood and rich soil that feed new sprouting saplings. Moisture, insects, and fungi break down sturdy tree fiber into pulp, which acts as a water-storage material for the soil.

Shield ferns (the overall shape and individual frond leaves are triangular) proliferate beneath mixed hardwoods of birch and oak.

The Sanbornton Boulder will delight restless children tired of driving in the car.

To the left of the trail a "boulder train" (stop 6) frozen in time seems to come plummeting down an embankment. These slides of rock from the White Mountains were carried and dropped here by a melting glacier 10,000–12,000 years ago. Boulder trains are clues to the direction of glacial ice movements.

Notice the stone wall to the right. Walls not only marked property boundaries in New England but also were a tidy way to clear pastureland. In this area red oak trees (stop 7) have been spared by loggers. Red oak yield fast-growing, durable lumber as well as produce acorns for red and gray squirrels and other small animals. Beaver, for instance, consider the inner bark of aspen fabulous while ruffed grouse love aspen buds for winter food. A short climb up an easy hill brings a monumental surprise—one of New Hampshire's largest free-standing boulders. A crack from weathering cleaves the granite, forming a tunnel-like passage that will delight exploring children, as will its nickname—"Paul Bunyan's Paperweight." The big boulder has a 93.5-foot waistline and is 25 feet tall.

Continue to the left of the Sanbornton Boulder, keeping above and behind the rest area. Traffic noise is pronounced, but it doesn't seem to squelch the chattering of towhees, catbirds, nuthatches, and other feathered residents.

Shortly beyond a picnic table and to the left grows a red pine (stop 10) easily identified by the pinkish red tinge of its bark and tall straight trunk.

To name a few picnic tables and restrooms beside a noisy interstate a "rest area" always seems like an oxymoron. However, this addition of a short nature trail adds a relaxing and informative element to the tedium of car travel. We hope the Sanbornton Rest Area becomes part of a statewide, if not national, trend.

Getting There

The Sanbornton Rest Area is found by driving south past Exit 22 on I-93. The trail is well marked at the top of a flight of steps to the right of the main building.

Other Information

RC&D Area Forester
Coop Extension Service
Conway, NH 03818

Hannah Dustin Memorial Historic Site

Merrimack River Memorial Trail
Penacook

- 0.4 mile
- 30 minutes
- easy

A short, intriguing walk over an old iron railroad trestle to a historic island monument.

Families will find this enjoyable for everyone. It's all here—birds, trees, a railroad bridge, rushing river waters, an island, views of old mills, a historic tale of early colonial wars, and a grassy open area around the statue of Hannah Dustin.

From the right rear corner of the parking lot, the macadam pathway leads straight down a gentle slope, passing young birch and beech on the left. At the bottom of the asphalt path, continue straight across an old road that leads to the left toward a dismantled section of a bridge over the wide Merrimack River.

Proceed straight through a sheltering small grove of young eastern red cedar, which is really a juniper, with very small, berrylike cones; scaly, thready bark; and tight, flat, waxy, needlelike leaves. Its wood is used for

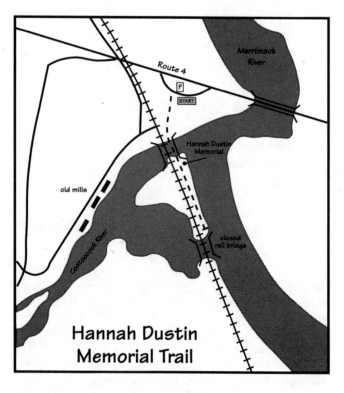

Hannah Dustin
Memorial Trail

pencils and chests, its distilled oil for soaps, perfumes, and insecticides.

The pathway is obvious. In fifty feet it takes you to the left of a high-sided iron railroad trestle bridge over the delta of the confluence of the Merrimack and Contoocook Rivers. At this point I-93 is visible to the left on the far side of the Merrimack River, which from here flows south toward Concord and the Atlantic Ocean.

The Merrimack (meaning in Indian language "swift water") remains a singularly important river in New Hampshire, draining the central section of the state and anchoring a vast watershed in this state and Massachusetts. In the early nineteenth century it was a cradle of. America's Industrial Revolution, as early entrepreneurs harnessed its steady hydropower to develop networks of textile mills. Today the Merrimack, badly polluted by 150 years of exploitation, is being restored to health with the help of such groups as the Merrimack River Watershed Association.

The Contoocook River, too, is singular, the only river in the state that flows north. It's a wonderfully peaceful river most of its length through the southwestern part of the state.

Follow the path alongside the trestle and straight along the abandoned railroad tracks to the open monument area now visible ahead.

If you continue past the statue down the path on the left of the tracks (return to the monument later), you'll soon see to the right the rush of the Contoocook as it bends toward you and the Merrimack. This is a good spot to look across the river at an old flour and corn mill with its red-brick buildings and smokestacks. The name Roller Flour Mill painted on one building is still legible.

In 1789 a sawmill was built nearby to take advantage of the strong water power. Other mills followed over the years, including a woolen mill in 1847. By 1873 Penacook village was producing more than 4 million yards of cotton print cloth, valued at $1.5 million a year. A flour mill was operating in 1858; at its heyday the mill operated twenty-four hours a day and could grind 5,000 bushels of corn one day and hundreds of barrels of flour the next.

Tree and shrub growth along the trail is varied and plentiful. This watery site is especially conducive for alder, the diminutive relative of the birches (both barks grow characteristic lenticels, the raised, horizontal ridges particularly noticeable on white birch). The spongy-soft stalks of staghorn sumac are easy to spot here, too, with their tendency to grow in clusters; their fuzzy, dark red, upright cone berries are plain to see. Sumac twigs have a dozen or more leaflets, whitish underneath. In fall, the leaves may "out red" the sugar maple. The poison sumac you may hear about are found in and near swamps and are distinguished by their yellowish white berries hanging downward: Don't touch! They produce allergic reactions like poison ivy.

Birds are plentiful, too; they like the surrounding water. One late spring we saw a yellow-and-black Baltimore oriole, flycatchers, a goldfinch, a fire-engine-red cardinal, red-winged (with yellow bar) blackbirds, squawky blue jays, and a kingfisher (a notable bird: with slate blue and white plumage, a large crested head, and a spearlike bill, it hovers unevenly over the water, then plunges down to nab its prey).

Often, it's better to let birds come to you instead of the reverse. Pick a spot, be quiet, be still, be patient. Birds are curious but cautious. Listen for chirps getting closer while you assure the birds you're no threat by making no sudden moves or sounds.

Another high steel-beam railroad trestle bridge ends the walk on the other side of this minuscule island where the Contoocook River flows directly into the Merrimack.

This railroad trestle bridge once linked an island and the bank of the Merrimack River.

Its mighty beams harken back to railroad traffic moving beside the wide-flowing New Hampshire rivers and through rich farmland and countryside. Instead of train whistles, now I-93 traffic noise prevails.

Returning to the monument, one can reflect on the story of Hannah Dustin. In March 1697, having just given birth to a child, she, her nurse, and her other children were abducted by Indians and forced to march north 150 miles from Massachusetts. The baby died. Late one night in April, Hannah rallied her nurse and other captives while their captors were asleep. With purloined hatchets in hand, they pounced upon the sleeping Indians and "struck such home-blows upon the heads of their oppressors that they fell down dead. The two women and the youth then followed the Merrimack back to Haverhill, carrying 10 scalps, for which they received a bounty of fifty pounds."

On the west side of the monument are etched the names of the escaped captives. On the south side reads:

Statua
"Know ye that we with many plant it
In trust to the statua we give and grant it
That the tide of time may never cant it
Nor Mar Nor Sever
That Pilgrims here may heed the mothers
That truth & faith & all the others
With banners high in glorious colors
May stand forever"

Getting There

From I-93 above Concord, take Exit 17 to U.S. 4 west. Drive about a half-mile to the large parking lot on the left for the Hannah Dustin Monument (open year-round).

Profile Falls
Recreation Area
Profile Falls Trail
Bristol

- **0.6 mile**
- **20 minutes**
- **easy**

*A short climb and descent to the base of a
forty-foot cascade in the Smith River.*

Whether they're thin streams or giant Niagaras, waterfalls elicit an extraordinary attraction, and Profile Falls is
no exception. Here the water falls on a diagonal, creating
a sheet of white water as Smith River tumbles over slabs
of granite.

The sound of thrashing water, the eternal tumble of
rivers over cliffs, the mesmerizing sense of unstoppable
motion—waterfalls create a basic human urge to see and
be near them.

It's easy to see and be near Profile Falls. From the
small parking alcove, the access trail begins at the back-
side of the lot at a clear break into the woods.

Walk between two boulders at a signless trailhead
and immediately cross a short footbridge.

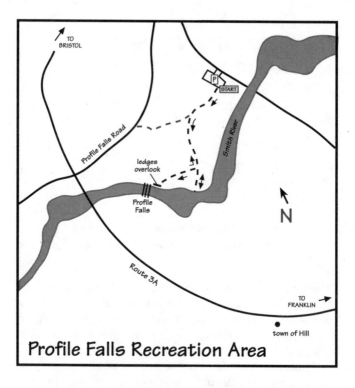

Profile Falls Recreation Area

Stay on the footpath to avoid poison ivy (three shiny leaves and a reddish stem low to the ground). Because it's a sun lover, poison ivy grows in profusion at certain points along open footpaths, especially near your favorite wild berry bushes, which like the sun, too. Mature poison ivy can use its aerial roots to climb tree trunks. (In the South and West, a variety of ivy called poison oak climbs up oak and other trees.) Poison ivy is particularly potent in early spring, when the new season urges the plants into fast growth and the poison oil is fresh in the plant.

If you do smudge the poison on exposed skin and you're deep in the woods, look for jewelweed. These waist-high, spindly plants with quarter-size, mostly orange blooms are said to counteract the itchy, blistery poison ivy rash. Simply rub the flowers or moisture from the stems directly onto the irritations. We had to try it once, and jewelweed does relieve the itching.

Proceed directly into the woods along a well-worn path, ascending slightly. Right away you pass staghorn sumac on the right with their upright fuzzy "horns" along thick branches. These parasol-shaped shrubs favor open areas, which they fill in fast, forming thickets of natural awnings. The long and narrow toothed leaves turn stoplight red in fall. The "staghorn" name comes from the resemblance of its velvety branches to new deer antlers.

Less than a hundred feet from the trailhead is a choice linden tree (also known as American basswood) on the right. The large leaves are heart shaped, with one curved side at the stem slightly asymmetrical. This is a good location to see the linden leaves low and up close. In a more open location this tree would spread into a comforting oval shade tree, and often it is planted as an ornamental in yards to provide shade.

In 300 feet you face a three-trail junction. Take the left fork and walk toward the faint sound of the waterfall. The trail descends somewhat, and in another 300 feet a sign, Profile Falls, points left and down a steep embankment to the river edge.

Before the main attraction tugs you onward, to the right off the trail about fifteen feet is a field-stone cellar hole, what's left of a homestead in earlier years.

Smith River is now in sight. The river churns below you, its rushing waters flowing around a grassy island of trees.

At the hillside edge, take the trail descending toward the right to the riverbank. Another trail connects as you proceed down this short distance, but take the lower branch close to the water for the best first view of the falls.

Walk to the edge of a peninsula that juts into Smith River, a good, low-level spot to see the curtain of white water rushing over the rock outcrop ahead.

Profile Falls.

Surrounding you on this strip of land grow a few hickory trees (five or seven toothed leaflets, the first pair from the tip usually the longest), white pine (five long needles to the cluster), maple (three-pronged leaves), and hemlock (short, flat needles in two flat rows). This makes a handy location to identify these stalwart trees.

Here, too, are silvery spleenwort ferns, with short, oblong, smooth pinnae (the leaflike part of the blade). These and other ferns thrive in moist forest areas such as those around Profile Falls. As part of the family of flowerless plants, ferns reproduce by spores in minute spore sacs located at various points on the frond, depending on the species.

Down low in front of the falls is a pleasant site to sit and relax on the lightly sprayed boulders.

On the way back up the short hillside trail, look this time on the left bank for some of the flora you missed on the way down. Notice the fir and hemlock seedlings trying to get a roothold on the riverbank, and the plentiful partridgeberry with its moderately scalloped, dark green leaves. A low-growing evergreen creeper, partridgeberry forms a carpet of green a few inches above ground. Its four-petaled white flowers bloom in pairs, which in the fall turn into paired red berries lasting through winter. The berries, also known as twinberries, are eaten by birds.

Once again on flat ground overlooking the river, make a U-turn toward the falls for a higher view. Stay clear of where the red warning sign says Steep Bluff & Loose Rock. Keep Back.

Move more to the right where you can climb through rocks in sparse evergreens to an even higher ledge overlooking the falls.

Return on the same trail to the parking lot.

Getting There

At Central Square in Bristol take NH 3A south. Clock 2.1 miles. On the right of NH 3A is a Heritage Trail sign prior to the left-hand turn onto Profile Falls Road. Drive 0.4 mile on Profile Falls Road and make a sharp right. Enter the gate to the recreation area. It is a bumpy 0.2 mile to the dirt parking lot, with Profile Falls trailhead on the right.

Other Information

Franklin Falls office telephone: 603-934-2116

Several trails and roads wind along the Smith River in the Profile Falls Recreation Area.

Wellington State Park

Peninsula Trail (Loop)

Bristol

- **1 mile**
- **45 minutes**
- **easy**

Walk through this red-pine forest sloping to the edge of the fingerlike peninsula on large Newfound Lake.

Popular lakes often lose their appeal when cottages, motorboats, and crowded conditions replace what nature had to offer in the first place. Fortunately, Newfound Lake still has some reserved sections of rich woodland on the lake shore that retain a sense of natural beauty and interest. This walk is one of them.

Look for a gate beside the restrooms building. Walking down this short dirt road to the trailhead, you'll discover a small marsh on the left and a series of rock ledges on a hillside to the right. These two distinct habitats create what foresters call "edge effect," where wildlife thrives on the diversity of habitats. For instance, on this short stretch we saw two mink. One of them slipped into a rock-crevice den while the other slid into the marsh pool and grasses on the other side. A visitor from the city told us she had seen "ferrets" earlier. A

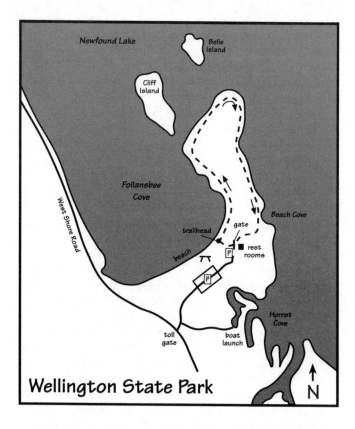

Newfound Lake

Belle Island

Cliff Island

Follansbee Cove

West Shore Road

Beach Cove

trailhead

gate

beach

P

rest rooms

P

Hornet Cove

toll gate

boat launch

Wellington State Park

N

park forester confirmed our suspicion that she had seen these mink, part of the weasel family. One of the many species and subspecies of the family is ermine, which grows to about fifteen inches long. In winter its luxurious coat turns protective snow white, except for the coal black tip of the tail. By extension, "ermine" also refers to other white-coated members of the weasel family.

Speckled alder grows in the marsh and enjoys getting its roots wet. A member of the birch family, this shrub has dark green shiny leaves and produces catkins. The clumped trunks have horizontal lenticels (dashlike marks) on their bark like their birch relatives. Catbirds and red-winged blackbirds chatter and call from these bushy speckled alder, found often in and around swamps and marshes.

Crescent Beach fronts Follansbee Cove. Turn right and pass a covered picnic pavilion. The park was built originally by President Franklin Delano Roosevelt's "tree army," the Civilian Conservation Corps (CCC), in the 1930s. To the right, on the eastern edge of the beach is a trailhead sign and memorial plaque to the CCC, also explaining that Elizabeth R. Wellington deeded the ninety-seven-acre peninsula to the state of New Hampshire for public use. Two-acre Belle Island was annexed to the park in 1931, and six-acre Cliff Island in 1933.

Follow orange blazes behind the signboard onto Peninsula Trail, which skirts the lake nearly the entire distance. Pine needles carpet the forest floor beneath the evergreens. Chickadees chatter and call from the hemlock and red pine. This is a lovely forest of many tall mature conifers, clear of undergrowth. The majestic red Norway pine trunks glow a healthy ruddy color. You can even hear the screams of seagulls that have flown inland to the coves on this deep, long trout-filled lake.

At 0.28 mile look beyond the rocky shore to discover an island in progress. Already, a tall tree has taken root in the soil formed from leaf debris washed into the crevices of the offshore boulders. Perhaps this is another habitat for a raccoon, sleek long otter diving for freshwater clams, or migratory warblers resting in the silvery leaves of the lone tree.

At 0.4 mile on the other side of a narrow channel lies Cliff Island. From a granite ledge jutting into the clear green water, you can contemplate the beauty of the southern reaches of Newfound Lake. Cliff Island is off-limits to park visitors on days when scouts and other groups camp there. Canoe convoys frequently head for nearby Belle Island. Watching the paddlers, it's easy to imagine early native Algonquins who camped on this lake and fished from six- and seven-man dugout canoes.

A boulder train spills down the steep hillside to the right of the trail, and at 0.5 mile is a convenient handrail and eastern view of Cliff Island. A few paces more and you graze the side of a whale-shaped leviathan boulder we affectionately named "Beluga."

A simple bench has been fashioned near another boulder. It faces a hillside of magnificent red Norway pine. Just beyond, a sign points to Belle Island. Both Belle and Cliff Islands once were known respectively as Pig and Hog Islands. In the nineteenth century much of New Hampshire was farmland, and, like coastal farmers, the local yeomen kept hogs and sheep on islands close to the shore.

As you round the peninsula, the sound of the water lapping against the eastern rocky shore suddenly adds another dimension to the walk. From a railing, you can see the steeples and white facades of the town of Bridgewater nestled on the opposite shore. At 0.7 mile stop on a stone causeway for another view of this picturesque

At Wellington State Park Norway pines and fjordlike coves leave a definite Nordic impression.

lakeside town. The conifers give way to birch and red oak. Mushrooms push through the loam beneath these deciduous trees. We identified a cluster of brilliant yellow waxy caps. The stems and caps are golden and shine like candles against the dark earth.

Beaver are active on the shoreline here, and the trees they don't topple are cleared by park foresters who recognize the value of an unobstructed lake view. If you haven't noticed the pencil-sharp tree stumps gnawed by the sharp-toothed beaver, a sign saying Beaver Activity points out some older stumps on the trailside.

From a sandy cove at about 0.8 mile, the trail doubles back and inland up a slope to the right.

Stone steps on the hillside (the equivalent of a flight of stairs) facilitate the climb. Another series of stone steps takes you down the other side to complete this dramatically picturesque peninsula loop.

Getting There

From Exit 23 on I-93, take NH 104 to Bristol. At Center Bristol near the post office on NH 104 still going west, turn north (right) onto NH 3A and drive 2.1 miles. Turn left onto West Shore Road (a sign to Wellington State Beach precedes this turn). Stay on West Shore Road (another road comes in at 1.7 miles and West Shore Road curves right). Turn right into the park at 2.7 miles. Drive past the rectangular beach parking lot to a shaded loop parking area on the left near the restrooms.

Other Information

No fee for use of the trail. The park is undeveloped to the west of Shore Road, but hikers may follow the Elwell Trail to Goose Pond and Sugarloaf Mountains.

Paradise Point Audubon Nature Center

Elwell & Lakeside Trails (Loop)

East Hebron

- **0.8 mile**
- **1 hour**
- **easy**

Fragrant hemlock forest and pristine shore meet at Paradise Point, a heavenly ledge lookout on Newfound Lake.

The walk begins behind the gate on the short road to the nature center. (No vehicles allowed except for the handicapped.)

At 0.1 mile you come to a two-room pine cabin that serves as the active focal point for summer-long nature and educational programs.

Deepening visitor interest and appreciation of the outdoors, the Paradise Point Audubon Nature Center makes an intriguing introduction to the trail. Be sure to spend some time here at this "priming station." It'll whet your appetite for learning more firsthand in the woods. Kids will enjoy the center, too.

Turtles sun in an aquarium, and on the porch a barred owl that has been an Audubon member for ten years stares at you with wondrous limpid eyes. A poster

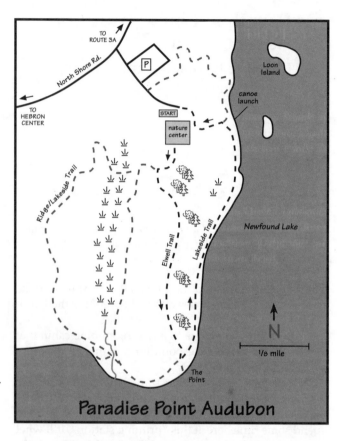

Paradise Point Audubon

on the wall pictures New England snakes and identifies the timber rattlesnake, a giant muscular king sheathed in a duff-and-brown diamond skin, as the only poisonous snake in New Hampshire. Several Rattlesnake Mountains and Rattlesnake Islands dot the New Hampshire map, but in several decades of hiking, climbing, and bushwhacking the southern forest where *Crotalus horridus* allegedly lives, we have yet to encounter this rattler.

The center encourages family participation and has many exhibits, nature puzzles, and games for young hands and eyes. While toddlers delight in the discoveries of the Feely Box, parents can read about the common loon and learn about the hieroglyphics of bark beetles.

Behind the nature center, follow the red and yellow blazes of the Ridge/Lake Trail fifty feet to the top of a knoll. Veer to the left at the junction. (The trail to the right is marked Elwell and leads to a marsh; this protected lakeside sanctuary was entrusted to the Audubon Society by the Elwell family.) The red blazes you follow now guide you along the part of the trail closest to the lake. Follow them into the hemlock forest and downhill. Look for patches of blue lake water through the hemlock boughs on your left. At times, unfortunately, motorboats introduce a discordant note conflicting with the silent majesty of hundred-year-old hemlocks. Visit midweek, early in the day, and you'll have more chance of enjoying this grove in peace.

In spring you pass by vernal pools where amphibians lay their eggs. By summer pools like these usually disappear, along with the frogs and salamanders, which migrate the short distance to the lake shore.

To the right of the trail a short distance before reaching Paradise Point grows a yellow birch propped up on its roots. This "giraffe tree" has sprouted a long neck trunk from several knobby airborne roots. The holes and crevices formed from shallow root systems like this provide shelter for moles, chipmunks, and larger forest inhabitants.

This birch has been nicknamed the "giraffe tree."

At 0.2 mile you arrive at the lake shore. Turn right, clamber over a huge red pine (reddish bark, straight trunk), and take the slope spur path down to Paradise Point. This ledge of granite provides an ideal spot for rest and a picnic, with great "photo ops" of picturesque, six-mile-long Newfound Lake.

Formed by glacial erosion, the lake reaches a depth of 180 feet, and its pure water is completely renewed two and a half times a year. Algonquin Indians camping on the shore called it *Pasquaney,* or "place where birch bark is found for canoes." Many sites have been discovered along with flint arrowheads and other tools that were made at these camps. During the nineteenth century, local farmers speared fish spawning in the lake and salted them in barrels. Today, fishermen troll for trout, bass, and pickerel. Sleek mink coats frequently are seen slipping in and out of the granite crevices, for this member of the weasel family also enjoys trout.

After walking back up the slope, turn right and follow the yellow blazes of the Lakeside Trail. The litter of rocks in the narrow path along the water rivets walkers' attention for awhile. At 0.4 mile you come to another overlook on the lake. (This prime forty-three-acre tract of land includes 3,500 feet along the pristine north shore.)

On the left pass a massive boulder and another one on the right about ten yards farther ahead. These granite monoliths are covered with several types of lichen. Foliose lichen present leaflike shapes, and umbilicate lichen have tiny cords attaching them to the rock. These odd growths really are formed by two organisms—algae and fungi—cohabiting in symbiotic harmony. British children's book author/illustrator Beatrix Potter discovered this dual cooperative structure when she was a young botanist. In *Plant Explorer's Guide to New England,* naturalist Raymond Wiggers suggests naming a species of lichen after her, since at the turn of the century her research was completely ignored because she was a woman.

At 0.7 mile, walk around a canoe rack. Turn left, walk up the hill to the right of the nature center, and then back to the parking lot. (You may also return to your car via a short loop trail that continues along the lake.)

Getting There

From the rotary junction of NH 3A and NH 25W, turn south (left) onto NH 3A and drive 5 miles. At the state sign, Sculptured Rocks, Paradise Point, Wellington State Beach, turn right and drive 1 mile on North Shore Road (no road sign). At 1.0 mile turn left onto Paradise Point access road and park.

Other Information

Canoeing, educational programs, environmental day camp, resource library, and professional naturalists. Trails open dawn to dusk. Nature center open 10:00 A.M. to 5:00 P.M. mid-June to Labor Day. Call 603-744-3516 for details. The Hebron Marsh Sanctuary is located down the road but has no trail; an observation platform is accessible for bird-watching on the lake.

Affiliated Organization

Audubon Society of New Hampshire
3 Silk Farm Road
Concord, NH 03301
603-224-9909

Sculptured Rocks Natural Area
Sculptured Rocks Trail
Groton

- **0.8 mile**
- **30 minutes**
- **easy**

A trail for sauntering into the quiet woods behind the Cockermouth River's narrows of convoluted, smooth rock .

The thundering of spring melt through the crimped canyon walls of Sculptured Rocks Natural Area shows the eventual triumph of water over granite. The constant flow of whitewater bashing the rock walls with river-borne stone and sediment for millennia has worn the sub-base smooth and hollow. It's a mesmerizing scene.

The short access trail from the parking lot to the site is marked. Follow the sign pointing across the road diagonally toward the right to a connector trail into the woods. Walk 100 feet to the narrow rock gorge that channels the river. You can't miss it.

A thirty-foot descent of the Cockermouth River through a cleft in the boulder-base earth has carved three-to-four-foot-deep potholes and scooped fantasy shapes.

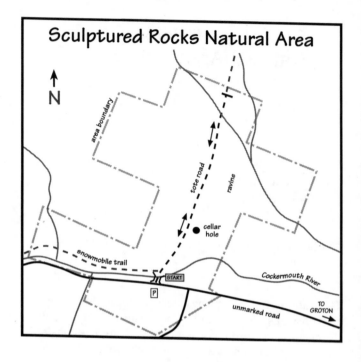

Sculptured Rocks Natural Area

N

area boundary

tote road

ravine

cellar hole

snowmobile trail

START

P

Cockermouth River

unmarked road

TO GROTON

The scene is surrounded by quaking aspen, hickory, hemlock, and other familiar mixed woods. Quaking aspen (also known as trembling aspen) is one of the fast-growing poplars that dangle catkins in spring before the leaves appear. The circular, fluttering, toothed leaves grow on extra-long, flattened stems and "tremble" in the downiest of breezes, creating a ruffling overhead. But trees are far from the main attraction here. Your eye catches the smooth ledges by the riverbank and your ear, the eternal rush of whitewater.

A fifty-foot-long, wire-mesh bridge over the gorge comes in sight another fifty feet to the right. Before crossing the bridge, to the right of it is a narrow footpath to the rocks below. This gets you close to the main attraction. Smooth natural boulder picnic tables may be loud from the thunderous water, but intriguing.

A trail (no blazes or sign) continues across the bridge and onto an earthen road into the forest. Ascend slightly (in spring the ground underfoot can be spongy); on the right in 300 feet pass an old cellar hole constructed from field stone. Who in years past thought to build a house near this special river ravine? They must have loved it here.

Continue up the gentle grade through maple and oak towering overhead and frilly ferns scattered below. Look for the spreading shield fern here, which grows not much more than two feet high. One identifying sign is the overall broad shape in comparison to its length from nearly the top to the bottom of the blade, like a triangular "shield." The lowest pinna grows downward next to the stipe (stem).

At 0.3 mile continue straight past a road junction on the right. Beyond this point more beech and white birch appear, enhancing the light by reflecting it from the tall pale tree trunks and thin canopy. Soon the wide trail flattens.

In another 0.1 mile, cross a small gurgling brook flowing over a flat ledge—a gentle, soothing scene. Other narrow cascades here drain the steep woodlands. This predisposes you to look at the smaller plants growing in this area. Indian cucumber root alongside the trail, for example, is common in moist woods in the Northeast. It is identified by two tiers of leaves and small white flowers in spring, bluish purple berries in the fall and grows about two feet high. The slender stem grows through two levels of long, whorled leaves (sometimes nine of them). The flower gets its name from the cucumber taste of the root.

The trail continues, but this brook makes a good end point. Return to the bridge on the same pathway. Covering the same ground need not be anticlimactic. Your perspective is reversed and you can enjoy plants and trees you missed on the first round.

The thirty-foot cascade of Cockermouth River has chiseled a gorge and sculpted the rocks smooth.

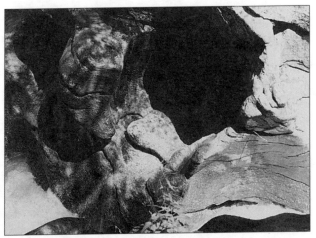

This view shows river-carved potholes that are three to four deep.

Getting There

From NH 3A turn onto NH 118 (West Shore Road; unmarked to Hebron and Groton). A sign indicates Paradise Point, Sculptured Rocks, Wellington State Park. Pass Newfound Lake Marina on the left to Hebron. At 2.4 miles continue on NH 118 to Groton. A sign indicates Sculptured Rocks. At 4.0 miles veer left at the sign. NH 118 turns sharply right. Drive 1.1 miles on this unmarked road and park in the lot to the left.

Cardigan State Park

West Ridge Cardigan Mount Summit Trail
Canaan/Orange

- **2 miles**
- **2 hours**
- **difficult**

The 3,121-foot bald peak of Cardigan Mountain offers hawk-eye views of the lakes region, the White Mountains, Vermont, and white Kinsman quartz veins underfoot.

The luck of the draw is that, unlike many other eastern states, New Hampshire has a fortuitous number of open summits. Cardigan Mountain is one of them. The hike up is relatively difficult, but if you like mountaintops, the rewards are extraordinary. (The AMC knows this, too: it has a year-round lodge at the foot of the mountain's east side. It's a wonderful place to stay, with comfortable bunk rooms, a roaring fire, and family-style meals.)

The summit of Cardigan is an extensive top-of-the-world perch of granite, a large bald unobstructed by shrubs or trees for a wonderful full-circle view.

Orange blazes and a sign for the West Ridge Trail designate the trailhead at the Cardigan Mountain parking lot.

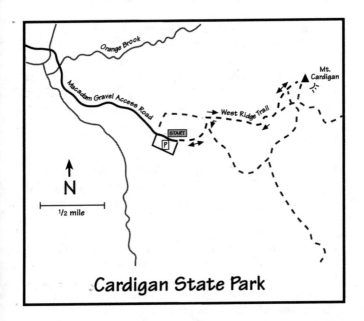

Cardigan State Park

The woods of mixed conifers, balsam fir, birch, and slender striped maples (also called moosewood) sparsely populate the upper slope. Snuggled near the smooth green trunks, hobblebushes seek the light along the trail. Their white "bridal wreath" bouquets decorate the woods in spring, turning to red berry clusters in autumn.

After a steady climb of 0.4 mile you come to an offshoot to Rimrock Trail, leaving right. Continue following the orange blazes up the west slope.

At 0.9 mile a graded, well-maintained flight of stone steps leads to a log bridge over a deep gulch. To the other side of the bridge is a clearing that looks like a tent site (although fires and camping aren't permitted on the trail). It provides a good resting place.

Overhead, a canopy of mountain ash shades the trail. It makes a favorite perch for the songbirds that eat the glowing red berries in the fall. The tree isn't an ash at all, but a member of the apple-hawthorn family. (The similar ornamental rowan tree seen on many New England lawns produces orange berries.)

After the bridge is a trail junction with a signboard to no fewer than eight different trails to various destinations. Follow the West Ridge Trail arrow to the left and up. Only a few more tenths of a mile brings you in sight of the summit fire tower.

The three-crested mass of granite in 5,655-acre Cardigan State Park has a five-mile base. This walk takes you up the 3,121-foot southern and main bald. Baldface, the middle peak of the Cardigan Mountain complex, has a sharp side nearly 1,200 feet perpendicular to the forest floor. Firescrew, the north peak, was named after a spiral of fire visible for miles during a devastating conflagration in 1855.

Perhaps the most salient feature on "Old Baldy," as the deforested summit affectionately has been dubbed, is a network of prominent veins of white quartz crisscrossing the granite bald in abstract geometric patterns. Known both as Clough (for the mines) and Kinsman (from the notch in the White Mountains near the mines), this metamorphic quartz formed from dramatic geologic upheaval 400 million years ago.

Because of the spectacular views, Cardigan is popular, especially on weekends and holidays. One Labor Day we heard excited children cry, "Bear!" as they

"Old Baldy" Cardigan is crisscrossed by veins of white metamorphic quartz.

peered into a boulder cave. But since we had passed fifteen dogs on leashes, most fauna, except the carefree vultures circling overhead, had disappeared.

The fire lookout accommodates as many visitors as can possibly fit into the small wind-whipped mountain penthouse. However, below the shaking scaffold, other attractions are worthy of examination. In the mossy microenvironments of rock crags and crannies near pools of collected rainwater grow mountain cranberries, five-petaled cinquefoil, and other alpine flowers.

Remember to bring your windbreaker, lots of drinking water, snacks, and binoculars.

Getting There

At Canaan from US 4 turn north onto NH 118 and drive 0.5 mile. At the State Park sign turn east onto Orange Road (at the fairgrounds). From here you see the bald of Cardigan Mountain. At 1.5 miles on Orange Road, you'll pass through the town of Orange. At 3.0 miles the road turns and winds over the remaining 1.5 miles of macadam and gravel road. At 4.0 miles is an Entering State Park sign. The parking lot perches on the west slope with lookouts for sunset viewing, picnic tables and pavilion, and pit toilets.

Other Information

New Hampshire Parks and Recreation
Box 856
Concord, NH 03302
603-271-3254

Dartmouth Outing Club Recreation Area

Appalachian Trail
Etna

- **1 mile**
- **1 hour**
- **moderate**

---

*This diverse section of the Appalachian Trail winds through
rich mixed woods, passes by a fern glade, crosses a brook,
skirts a meadow, and ends at an old cellar hole.*

Although walking this one-mile section of the renowned
Appalachian Trail leaves you with about 2,000 miles left
to hike, setting heel to the legendary "footpath through
the wilderness" connects you to extraordinary outdoor
history.

   The Appalachian Trail was principally the brainchild
and dream-come-true of Benton MacKaye, who pro-
posed this continuous footpath along the Appalachian
Mountain Range in an article in the *Journal of American
Institute of Architects* in 1921. The article so ignited interest and enthusiasm in members of existing outdoor and
hiking clubs that by the following year the first mile had
been marked and opened—in the Palisades Interstate
Park in New York. Three years later the Appalachian Trail

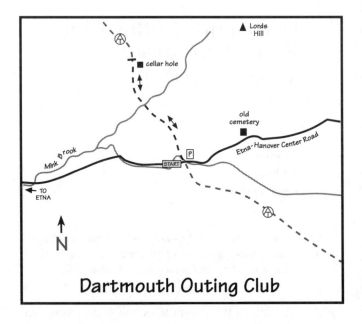

Dartmouth Outing Club

Conference was organized; by 1937 more than 1,200 blazed miles completed the route. Since then 800 miles have been added to avoid urban encroachments. Today, with the help of thousands of volunteers, the Appalachian Trail is maintained, sustained, and enjoyed by millions of people.

The Appalachian Trail, or AT, passes through fourteen states from Georgia to Maine—prime backcountry of mountain and meadows, rushing rivers and casual brooks. It was recognized as a National Scenic Trail under the National Trails Systems Act of 1968. In our judgment, this section of the trail in far western New

Hampshire, near where the AT crosses the Connecticut River from Vermont, is a delight.

Enter the trail on the cemetery side of the road and proceed down slightly onto a pine-needle-covered path under a variety of evergreens. The Dartmouth Outing Club uses orange blazes and keeps this section of the Appalachian Trail in top-notch shape; the AT is blazed in white vertical rectangle blazes.

Right away you approach an open area filled with graceful ferns. Then 100 feet into the trail, the soft rippling sounds of Mink Brook waft from the left through the woods before you see the stream. In another 200 feet the brook appears as it winds its way through the woodlands. To cross the brook, walk along the shore 10 feet to the left, where rocks make the crossing dry and easy.

But before you leapfrog across, note a cluster of ostrich ferns growing at the cross point. The fronds of the ostrich fern grow more than five feet high, although they don't appear so tall when they bend over in their natural state. Hold one of the fronds upright to see its full length as well as its shape, which is likened to a real ostrich plume. Ostrich fern fronds start at the base with small leaflike pinnae spaced widely from each other, then growing closer as they graduate up the stem. Toward the middle of the frond, the pinnae "leaves" grow longer and more crowded together until at about three-quarters to the tip the frond becomes very dense, wide, and full bodied. The end of the frond quickly curves to a short pointed tip.

After the brook, the trail continues through rich, spacious woods. In about a hundred feet after the brook, a giant dead "snag" remains standing on the right and

Snags (standing dead trees) provide nooks and crannies for chipmunks, red squirrels, owls, and other forest dwellers.

then come two huge white pine on the left, so large in comparison with nearby trees you can't miss them.

When we were walking the trail, at this point a well-outfitted hiker with a hefty new pack and solid, worn boots marched toward us. He turned out to be "Double Eagle," his Appalachian Trail moniker. Traditionally, thru-hikers on the AT adopt trail names. The name he made for himself derived from being both an Eagle Boy Scout and a retired marine colonel, both represented by an eagle insignia.

We struck up a conversation, talking to Double Eagle about our own thru-hike of the Appalachian Trail several decades ago, sharing camping stories, mosquito strategies, and constant thoughts of food. Double Eagle was hiking south to north, as we did, and encountered some of the same problems and delights of hiking the AT in a single four-month period. He recounted how helpful people were to thru-hikers along the trail, how friendly and interested they had been to him. Most of all, he said, he noticed how different trail life was from the polluted, crime-ridden metropolitan areas.

We assured Double Eagle that plenty of wonders awaited him in his last two states, that the view-packed Presidential Range of the White Mountains in New Hampshire ahead was as engrossing as boulder-laden Mahoosuc Notch in Maine was challenging.

Then Double Eagle went his way, we ours.

Nine hundred feet from the Etna trailhead, you leave the woods to skirt a large meadow of waist-high grasses, with yarrow and field daisies abounding in midsummer. Wild cherry and apple trees grow on the edge of the woodlands on the left.

At the corner edge of the field, follow the trail left, crossing the brook right away, and re-enter the mixed forest, passing more large white pine on the left and huge granite boulders on the right.

Ascend a hillside to a flat section at 0.25 mile. You'll notice how clear the trail is here. Continue another short section of easy ascent, reaching another flat area.

At 0.42 mile, turn left onto a flat, wide stretch with a stone wall on the right. Catbirds and chickadees seem at home in this area during summer.

At 0.46 mile veer right at a Y junction if you wish to continue a little more. Or stop here to muse upon the large cellar hole of an old farmstead on the right (be careful of rusted barbed wire).

Return to the trailhead on the same trail.

Getting There

From the Etna post office in Etna, drive on Etna Road (Main Street or Hanover Center Road) north 0.9 mile to the town cemetery on the left. You'll see a signpost and orange and white blazes on tree trunks where the trail crosses the road very close to where you approach the cemetery. Park on the side of the road.

Plummers Ledge
Geologic Site
Plummers Ledge Trail
Wentworth

- **0.4 mile**
- **20 minutes**
- **moderate**

Several prime examples of natural geologic potholes accessible for viewing from below and above.

For those serious about examining geological potholes firsthand, this excursion offers some large and small specimens. Be prepared to drive on mostly unidentified backcountry roads and to face less-than-adequate trail maintenance. When you do arrive at the site adjacent the road, little walking is required to see these examples of geological curiosities.

Two large, cavelike "potholes" next to each other at the base of a small geological upthrust measure fifteen feet each across. On top of the upthrust are three smaller potholes that are easy to reach.

Potholes are evidence of the endless process by which the earth's surface is first built up, then eroded over time. About 400 million years ago the granite you see here was a hot, molten liquid. Pressed upward from

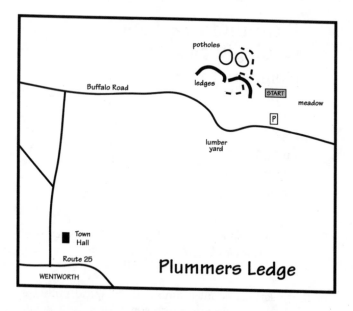

Plummers Ledge

deep within the earth, it extruded through softer sedimentary rock that had formed from the deposits on an ancient ocean floor. During the millennia of erosion that followed, water wore away the softer sedimentary rock, leaving the harder granite that we see revealed now. This set up the later geological developments of glaciation that left holes rubbed smooth and sculptured—the long-term power of water over stone. The potholes were worn into the granite from the abrasive effect of trapped water and gravel swirling over the rock.

Begin the footpath at a break in the corner edge of the woods fifty feet to the right as you face a sign nailed high on a tree: Plummers Ledge Geologic Site.

A modest-size clearing beside the dirt road takes you through bracken ferns, lowbush blueberries, and maple-leaf viburnum, a shrub tricky to identify in early summer because its leaves resemble the three-point leaves of red maple saplings. In autumn the differences are clear because the viburnum flower cluster between the opposite-stemmed leaves turns into purple berries.

At the trailhead bunchberries low to the ground are noticeable for the symmetry of their four petals, similar to the blossoms of the dogwood tree (bunchberry is, in fact, a member of the dogwood family). Both plants have bracts, which are more leaflike than the "flower" part it appears to be. The white flowers of early summer turn to bunches of reddish berries in the fall, giving the plant its name as well as quick identification.

Geological potholes at Plummers Ledge.

Follow the trail in a partial spiral around the edge of this little hill and veer left and down at a Y junction at a small rock bank. This portion of the trail takes you to a spot above the cliff where two large vertical potholes can be seen in the cliff wall. Below is the road you took that curves around the outcrop to the trailhead.

At an extra-large white pine, turn to the left to see these large potholes. To the right and down about thirty feet, you can walk to the base of the second pothole and see the obvious concave geological sculpture.

Return to the Y junction and take the left direction of the trail junction (the one you didn't take before), climbing 100 feet up to the flat top of the knoll.

After climbing over fallen tree trunks across the trail (volunteer scouts or other local crews are needed here), you reach the top of the cliff. Beds of bristly club moss (a tiny vertical series of plants) and running pine club moss (the miniature pine tree-looking ground cover) soften this section underfoot—providing a good picnic carpet.

Here on top of the hill are three small, natural geological potholes. One measures 2x2 feet and another beside it 3x3 feet; both are about 2 feet deep. The third pothole located to the left and 8 feet toward the cliff measures 4x5 feet. Most are filled with leaves and rainwater.

From this vantage point you can see the larger potholes down next to the road.

Descent down by the same trail, taking the left fork at the previous Y junction and following the path to the trailhead near the parking clearing.

Getting There

On NH 25 west before entering the village of Wentworth, look for Shawnees gas station/store. Take the first road to the right after Shawnees and drive past the Town Hall. You'll soon pass a lumber operation. Drive 0.4 mile and veer right at a Y junction onto Buffalo Road. At 2.7 miles the road becomes hard-packed dirt. Cross a bridge at 3.0 miles. On the left are granite ledges in the trees. Drive around the bend and park at 3.2 miles in the clearing on the left across from Precision Lumber yard.

Walks and Highlights

Region	Walk	Page Number	Difficulty Level	Distance (miles)
East	Bellamy River	1	easy	1.2
	Blue Job Mtn.	7	moderate	1
	Oak Hill	12	moderate	1
	NH Farm Museum	16	easy	0.5
	Branch Hill	21	easy	1.2
	Cooper Cedar Woods	25	easy	0.9
	Weeks Woods	30	moderate	1.75
	Mt. Major	35	difficult	2.5
	Powder Mill	42	easy	0.8
	Shaker Village Turning Mill Pond	50	easy	1.0
	Shaker Village Meadow Pond	59	moderate	1.8
	Lang Pond	66	moderate	3.0
	Knights Pond	73	moderate	2.4
	Lake Wentworth	79	easy	0.5
	Abenaki Tower	84	easy	0.3
	Russel Chase Bridge	88	easy	0.75
	Squam Lake	92	moderate	1.2

River or Brook	Lake or Pond	Swamp	Beach	Scenic Vista	Plants	Geology	Birds
✔				✔	✔		✔
				✔		✔	✔
						✔	
					✔		✔
✔					✔		
		✔			✔	✔	
				✔			
	✔			✔	✔	✔	
✔	✔		✔				
✔	✔			✔	✔		✔
✔	✔	✔		✔	✔		✔
	✔	✔	✔	✔	✔		✔
	✔	✔	✔	✔			✔
✔		✔	✔	✔	✔		✔
	✔			✔			
✔	✔						
	✔		✔	✔	✔		✔

Region	Walk	Page Number	Difficulty Level	Distance (miles)
East	Sidney Smith	97	moderate	0.9
	Hoyt Audubon	102	moderate	1.75
	Castle Springs Falls of Song	109	easy	0.25
	Castle Springs Pond	115	easy	0.75
	Markus Audubon	121	moderate	1.6
	Thompson Audubon	127	easy	0.6
	White Lake	132	easy	2.4
	Holderness Science Ctr. Gephart Trail	138	easy	1.0
	Holderness Science Ctr. Ecotone Trail	145	difficult	1.4
	Madison Boulder S.P.	151	easy	0.2
West	Rollins State Park	155	moderate	1.4
	Medicine Woods	162	easy	0.25
	Gardener Wayside Old Mill	169	easy	0.22
	Gardener Wayside Butterfield Pond	173	moderate	0.87
	Philbrick-Cricenti Bog	178	easy	0.75
	Lake Solitude	185	moderate	2.0

River or Brook	Lake or Pond	Swamp	Beach	Scenic Vista	Plants	Geology	Birds
	✔	✔			✔		✔
✔	✔	✔		✔	✔	✔	✔
✔				✔	✔	✔	
	✔		✔		✔		✔
✔	✔	✔			✔		✔
✔		✔		✔	✔		✔
	✔	✔	✔	✔	✔		✔
							✔
				✔	✔	✔	✔
✔					✔	✔	
				✔		✔	
					✔		
✔					✔	✔	
	✔	✔		✔	✔		✔
		✔		✔	✔		
	✔			✔	✔	✔	

Region	Walk	Page Number	Difficulty Level	Distance (miles)
West	John Hay N.W.R.	190	moderate	1.0
	Stoney Brook	196	easy	1.0
	Meriden Bird Club	202	moderate	1.4
	Saint-Gaudens Ravine Trail	210	easy	0.3
	Saint-Gaudens Blow-Me-Down	217	mod./diff.	2.0
	Clay Brook	224	easy	0.75
	Daniel Webster	229	easy	0.5
	Franklin Falls Dam	236	moderate	1.8
	Sanbornton Boulder	242	easy	0.3
	Hannah Dustin	247	easy	0.4
	Profile Falls	253	easy	0.6
	Wellington S.P.	259	easy	1.0
	Paradise Point	265	easy	0.8
	Sculptured Rocks	271	easy	0.8
	Mt. Cardigan	276	difficult	2.0
	Dartmouth Outing	281	moderate	1.0
	Plummers Ledge	287	easy	0.4

River or Brook	Lake or Pond	Swamp	Beach	Scenic Vista	Plants	Geology	Birds
	✔		✔	✔	✔		✔
		✔			✔		✔
		✔					✔
✔					✔	✔	
✔	✔			✔	✔		✔
✔					✔	✔	
✔					✔		✔
	✔			✔	✔	✔	
					✔	✔	
✔				✔			✔
✔				✔		✔	
	✔		✔	✔			
	✔	✔	✔	✔	✔		
✔						✔	
			✔			✔	
✔					✔		✔
						✔	

About the Authors

STEVE SHERMAN is the author of *Country Roads of New Hampshire* and *Country Roads of Connecticut/Rhode Island*. He co-authored (with Julia Older) *Nature Walks in Southern New Hampshire*.

JULIA OLDER'S third poetry collection *Higher Latitudes* explores man's connections with nature. With Steve Sherman, she co-authored *Appalachian Odyssey*, an account of their walk on the Appalachian Trail.

About the AMC

Since 1876, the Appalachian Mountain Club has promoted the protection, enjoyment, and wise use of the mountains, rivers, and trails of the Northeast. The AMC believes that successful, long-term conservation depends on first-hand experience and enjoyment of the outdoors. The AMC is a nonprofit organization whose membership of more than 72,000 members enjoy hiking, canoeing, skiing, walking, rock climbing, bicycling, camping, kayaking, and backpacking, while—at the same time—help to safeguard the environment. All AMC programs and facilities are open to the public.

AMC Huts & Lodges
AMC offers unique overnight lodgings throughout the Northeast. Spend an overnight at one of eight huts, each a day's hike apart, in the White Mountains of New Hampshire, or drive to Bascom Lodge atop Mount Greylock in western Massachusetts. Also accessible by car are Pinkham Notch Lodge or Crawford Hostel in New Hampshire, and Mohican Outdoor Center in the Delaware Water Gap of western New Jersey.

AMC Outdoor Adventures
Whether you're new to the outdoors or an old hand, the AMC offers workshops and guided trips that will teach you new skills, refine your expertise, or just get you outside in good company. Choose from more than 100 workshops and adventures offered. Whether you're

going solo, with your family and kids, or with friends, there is something for everyone.

Each of our 11 chapters—from Maine to Washington, D.C.—offers hundreds of activities close to home. Chapter leaders arrange hiking and bicycling trips and teach the basics of cross-country skiing, whitewater and flatwater canoeing, and other outdoor skills.

Volunteering

If you like to hike, discover the lasting satisfaction that comes with volunteering to maintain or build trails. No experience is necessary—we'll teach you what you need to know. The AMC leads volunteer trail building and maintenance crews throughout the Northeast. Our professional and volunteer crews take great pride in maintaining 1,400 miles of trails throughout the region.

Paddlers can help clean up a river, monitor water quality, or help negotiate access with private landowners. Volunteering is a great way to give something back to the rivers and trails that have taken you to so many wonderful places.

Conservation Leadership

Much of the northeast's outdoor recreation opportunities would not be possible without a commitment to protecting land and keeping trails, rivers, and mountains accessible. Since its founding, the AMC has been at the forefront of the conservation movement. AMC members fought for the creation of the White Mountain National Forest in 1911. More recently we have been active in protecting the Appalachian Trail corridor, improving access to and the health of rivers and land around hydroelectric dams, and improving water and air quality. Our conservation policies are backed by solid scientific research, conducted by our own professional researchers in conjunction with organizations such as the Harvard School of Public Health, Dartmouth College, U.S. Forest Service, and the National Park Service. We're working to keep our air clean and healthy, our waterfalls clear, our rivers running free, and recreational activities open.

AMC Books & Maps

The AMC publishes an extensive line of books, including nature guides, New England history, outdoor skills, conservation, and our famous trail guides and maps. AMC guidebooks are essential companions for all kinds of outdoor adventures throughout the eastern U.S. Our publications are available at most bookstores and outdoor retailers as well as our main office in Boston and Pinkham Notch Visitor Center in New Hampshire. To order by phone, call 800-262-4455. Also available through the AMC is *Appalachia*, the country's oldest mountaineering and conservation journal.

AMC Membership

We invite you to join the Appalachian Mountain Club and share the benefits of membership. Your membership includes a one-year subscription to *AMC Outdoors*—the Northeast's premier outdoor recreation magazine—keeping you informed on conservation issues. Members also enjoy discounts on AMC books, maps, workshops, and lodgings, as well as free affiliation to one of AMC's eleven chapters.

For more information on AMC, call 617-523-0636. To join, send a check for $40 for an adult, or $65 for a family to AMC Membership, 5 Joy Street, Boston, MA 02108; or if you prefer to pay by Visa or MasterCard, call 617-523-0636.

Alphabetical Listing of Areas